Martial Arts™

the
Tae Kwon Do
handbook

Martial Arts™

^{the}
Tae Kwon Do
handbook

Mark and Ray Pawlett

ROSEN
PUBLISHING®

New York

We would like to dedicate this book to our family and the memory of Damian Smethurst. A Tae Kwon Do instructor should respect his students and treat them as part of an extended family. Damian was part of my extended family and will be missed.

Aymez Loyaulte

This North American edition published in 2008 by:

The Rosen Publishing Group, Inc.
29 East 21st Street
New York, NY 10010

North American edition, this format, printed in 2008 by The Rosen Publishing Group, Inc.

Creative Director: Sarah King
Project Editor: Judith Millidge
Photographer: Colin Bowling
Designer: Axis Desing

Library of Congress Cataloging-in-Publication Data

Pawlett, Mark.
The tae kwon do handbook / Mark and Ray Pawlett.
— North American ed.
     p. cm. — (Martial arts)
Includes index.
ISBN-13: 978-1-4042-1396-8 (library binding)

1. Tae kwon do—Juvenile literature. I. Pawlett, Raymond. II. Title.
GV1114.9.P38 2008
796.815'3—dc22
                                                                2007031559

Manufactured in the United States of America

Contents

Introduction

Tae Kwon Do is a Korean martial art that employs mainly kicking, punching, striking, and evasive techniques. It has been developed from a unique historical and philosophical background.

In this book we will examine the history, philosophy, techniques, and teaching of Tae Kwon Do. The reader will gain an insight into Tae Kwon Do and a few new ways of viewing the art.

Mark Pawlett has a second Dan black belt from the WTF (World Tae Kwon Do Federation) style of Tae Kwon Do. He has studied the art at its spiritual home of Korea. He also holds a science PhD and has an intimate knowledge of the workings of the human body.

Ray Pawlett has studied Tae Kwon Do for several years. His main style of martial art is Tai Chi, for which he was the British Open Champion in 1999. He is also a healer, using the traditional Japanese method of Shiatsu. By profession he is an engineer, thereby adding a level of pragmatism to the mix.

The two authors have a vast range and depth of experience and knowledge in the field of traditional martial arts. They hope to convey some of that knowledge to the reader.

A word of warning

The techniques in this book have been selected from traditional Tae Kwon Do training and modern scientific sports training. Every effort has been made to ensure that all the techniques and methods described are accurate and safe.

Tae Kwon Do is a physical art. In every physical movement skill, whether it is martial arts, dance, or sports, there is an element of risk. Ultimately, the person who is responsible for managing that risk is you.

It is all too easy to misunderstand the written word, and this could result in injury if you are unlucky. Also, the exercises and training tips in the book may not suit your individual requirements. For this reason, it is vital that you consult your instructor before taking up the training described in this book. If you are still in doubt, consult a doctor or qualified practitioner.

The techniques and applications described are real. Under no circumstances should you attempt the two-person training techniques unless your instructor agrees that you are ready for it.

All the techniques require training and practice. Even the most basic-looking techniques will have multiple layers of complexity. Do not think that simply reading a Tae Kwon Do book teaches you self-defense. For that, you will need qualified instruction. Always try to walk away from a confrontational situation whenever you can.

Chapter 1 **The development of martial arts**

In prehistoric times *Homo Sapiens* evolved instincts to preserve their own lives and that of their species. The tools they used to defend themselves were primarily the most basic available—weapons of the body, such as the hands and feet.

Throughout the animal kingdom, fighting skills were honed by a combination of factors, from natural instincts, to observing confrontational situations, and by trial and error. Animals, and to a certain extent human beings, rely on their instincts. The development of fighting or martial skills is based on humankind's natural desire for self-preservation.

With the evolution of fighting techniques, some participants naturally became more proficient than others, either for reasons of physical advantage or simply because they acquired more experience. These men (and in early societies it was almost always men) became the warriors or soldiers, responsible for protecting fellow members of their tribe or family from outside danger.

The warrior's job was to fight. This would mean that the warrior would constantly have to think about his or her own mortality. Around the world different concepts developed whereby the warrior would learn to accept the possibility of his own death and not fear it.

The fighting concept has changed from being a fighting skill to something that is more spiritual. Fear of death is one of the primordial fears of all living beings, and learning to accept that fear has a deep spiritual effect. The way of the warrior is now as much about spiritual content as it is about learning to fight efficiently. One manifestation of this "way" is the study of martial arts.

The word "way" translates as "Do" in Korean. Learning a martial art like Tae Kwon Do enables students to study the "way" or "Do" of the warrior and also to learn about themselves.

Tae Kwon Do

Tae Kwon Do developed from Korean martial arts that date back more than 5,000 years. The Korean peninsula was often unsettled by tribal warfare, as well as incursions from neighboring countries. During ancient times, both the Mongols and Chinese Manchu Ch'ing dynasty invaded the Korean peninsula.

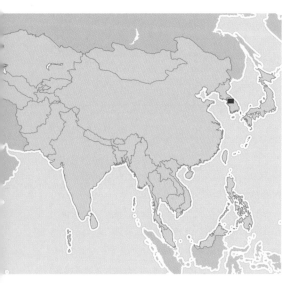

The Korean peninsula was open to invasion from both land and sea.

The Three Kingdoms period (40 BCE to 6th century CE) was a particularly important time for the development of Korean martial arts. As the name suggests, the Korean peninsula was mainly comprised of three kingdoms: Koguryo, Paekje, and Silla. They were constantly fighting to gain control of the Korean peninsula and dominance over each other. Each kingdom had its own kings and tribal chiefs and, consequently,

their own military training systems. It is through this constant rivalry that early Korean martial arts began to develop. Korean martial arts developed in this era include Subak (or Taekkyon), Sonbae, Soobakhee, Soobyuk, Beekaksool, Soobyukta, and Kwonbub.

The term "Tae Kwon Do" is composed of three parts: *Tae* means "foot," "leg," or "to step on"; *Kwon* means "fist" or "fight"; and *Do* means "the way or discipline." Modern Tae Kwon Do refers to a fighting system developed by the Koreans over many years that uses the hands and feet to deliver high-energy impact techniques for survival in confrontational situations. These techniques take the form of punches, strikes, kicks, and blocks. In any aggressive situation, the mind should remain peaceful, and the martial artist should recognize that the true enemy might be his or her own aggression.

Today, the Korean martial art of Tae Kwon Do shares similarities with many other Asian martial arts. Countries surrounding Korea, such as Japan and China, have influenced the evolution of Tae Kwon Do. Despite this evolutionary history, Tae Kwon Do is very distinct from other Asian martial arts. Tae Kwon Do is dynamic in both its evolution and performance, and this dynamic nature is often reflected in the lives and minds of Korean citizens. Tae Kwon Do has now developed into an international sport and is recognized as such by the IOC (International Olympic Committee).

The history of Korea and Tae Kwon Do

In Korean folklore Hwanung, the son of the Lord of Heaven, descended from heaven in the year 2333 BCE. Hwanung appeared under a sandalwood tree with 3,000 servants and established a City of God on the summit of the mountain Taebaeksan. A bear and a tiger wished to become human and so approached Hwanung to perform this transformation. Hwanung told them that to become human, they must avoid the sun for 100 days surviving on a diet of garlic and mugwort, which he had given them as a gift. The tiger failed the test, but the bear succeeded and emerged from the cave as a young woman. She mated with Hwanung and produced a son named Tan'gun, who became the first Korean king. Tan'gun established the country's capital at Pyongyang and thereby became the founder of Choson (ancient Korea), which is translated as "the land of the morning calm." The modern name Korea was derived from Koryo, which, in turn, was derived from Koguryo.

The origins of Korea are now thought to go back as far as 30,000 BCE. Nomadic Chinese established trading posts near Pyongyang during the Han dynasty. Constant wars with the Chinese necessitated an alliance between the besieged tribes of the north. Following the demise of the Han, the remaining tribes united in 37 BCE to form the first Korean kingdom of Koguryo. By the 3rd century CE the kingdoms of Silla and Paekje had formed in the south. During this time Korean culture was strongly influenced by China.

The Three Kingdoms period (37 BCE to 7th century CE)

Koguryo Kingdom (37 BCE to 68 CE)

King Dong Myeong Sung founded the Koguryo kingdom in 37 BCE. Koguryo consisted of a nomadic tribe comprised of five clans, collectively known as the Buye. Koguryo was able to remain independent despite constant threats from the Han dynasty of China. Evidence of Korean martial arts has been found in royal tombs and is evident from stone sculptures from the Koguryo period, such as the famous examples at Sokkuram Grotto.

The Koguryo developed a fighting art called Subak, and the practitioners were known as Sonbae, which translates as "a man of virtue who never recoils from a fight." Subak was handed down to the Hwarang warrior group of Silla. The martial art of Bak Sool ("head-butting techniques") was also developed during the Koguryo period.

Silla Kingdom (37 BCE to 935 CE)

The Silla Kingdom was founded by Park Hyuk Kusae in 37 BCE and lasted until 935 CE. Silla consisted of six clans collectively known as the Han. The Hwarang (translated as "flower knight") was an organization formed for the training and education of the Silla military elite. An instructor of the Hwarang, the monk Won Kwang Bupsa was also the author of the *Sesokokye*, a book that contains the philosophy of the Korean martial arts.

The king selected the Hwarang through contest. Military training of the Hwarang

included Subak (Taekkyon), fencing, horse riding, Dukgyon, Kkaekumjil, Ssirum (Korean wrestling), and education. Such training enabled the Silla to survive conflicts with the kingdoms of Koguryo and Paekje. Martial arts were also developed as the foundation of sports and were an important factor in deciding social class and position.

Paekje Kingdom (18 BCE to 660 CE)

The Paekje tribe fled from Koguryo and settled in the Han River basin. The Paekje kingdom was formed in 18 BCE by the leader Onjo and lasted until 600 CE. As in the other kingdoms, martial arts played an important part in national defense. The martial art of the Paekje was known as the Soo Sa system (which was similar to the Hwarang do organization of the Silla Dynasty).

Unified Kingdoms

The three kingdoms were almost constantly at war with each other, often allied with China or Japan, who were always looking for opportunities to rule the peninsula. The Three Kingdoms period came to an end in the 7th century when the Tang dynasty of China allied with Silla rulers to dominate the Korean peninsula. Fighting skills developed by the Silla enabled them to defeat the Paekje in 660 and the Koguryo in 668. The ruler of the Tang dynasty planned to establish hegemony over Korea. The Silla aristocracy then formed an

alliance with the remaining Koguryo and forced out the Chinese in 676, thus uniting the peninsula. Korea developed many aspects of its culture during the United Kingdoms period. As Buddhism spread, a variety of distinctive temples, tombs, and gardens was constructed. The relics of this development can be seen around Gyeongju, the former capital of Silla.

The Koryo dynasty (918–1392)

The Silla kingdom controlled the Korean people through military power, and this system inevitably created discontent. Eventually, warlords threatened the Silla leader, and power was passed to the ruler of the Koguryo without conflict. Wang Keon formed the new Koryo dynasty in 918 CE. During this period, Buddhism and Confucianism existed together, and military officers no longer had control over the country.

The martial art of Subak developed during the Koryo dynasty, and training included competition fights. International trade flourished, as did cultural exchanges with neighboring states, and Subak was an enduring export.

The Yi dynasty (1392–1910)

Invasion of Korea by the Mongols, led by Ghengis Khan in 1231, eventually led to the downfall of the Koryo dynasty. The Koryo monarch was overthrown in 1392, making way for the Yi dynasty. During the Yi dynasty, Buddhism was suppressed in favor of Confucianism. One factor contributing to the

decline of Buddhism was the deterioration in the popularity of Korean martial arts. People who practiced martial arts were considered inferior. It was considered better to spend time on other activities that were apparently more sophisticated, such as reading and writing poetry.

During the reign of Sejong the Great, there was vast cultural progress. Books were printed on medicine and astronomy, scholars such as Yi Hwang (T'oe Gye) and Yi Yi (Yul Gok) developed theories of the universe, and the new Korean script, Hangeul, led to a vast increase in literacy.

Subak became the people's martial art during the Yi dynasty. Deok Moo Lee and Jac Ka Park published the first Korean martial arts book named *Muyedobo-tongji* during the reign of King Jungjo. This book contains hand-fighting techniques resembling today's Poomsae (forms). Detailed hand drawings of each Subak technique are shown, as well as a clear description of the principles of the art.

Buddhism became more widespread in Korea during the political stability of the United Kingdoms period and under the Koryo dynasty, 676–1392.

Modern times

In 1910, the Japanese annexed Korea, abolished the monarchy, and ended the Yi dynasty. Remnants of the Korean army were driven out to Manchuria, Shanghai, and Hawaii, and Koreans had very little freedom. Many aspects of Korean culture, such as the Korean language and martial arts, were prohibited and replaced with Japanese. Korean martial arts were often practiced in secret.

After World War II, Japanese soldiers surrendered to the USSR in the north and the USA in the south. The dividing line between North and South Korea was the 38th parallel. The occupation of the Korean peninsula by the

The recent history of Tae Kwon Do

1	1961	Korean Tae Kwon Do Association (KTA) forms.
2	1962	Korean Tae Kwon Do Association joins Korea Athletic Society as a member organization.
3	1971	Dr. Un Yong Kim elected president of the Korean Tae Kwon Do Association (KTA).
4	1971	Tae Kwon Do is selected as Korea's national sport.
5	1972	Kukkiwon (National Skills Institute) is founded.
6	1973	The World Tae Kwon Do Federation (WTF) is founded.
7	1973	The 1st World Tae Kwon Do Championship Games take place.
8	1974	The first Asian Tae Kwon Do Championships take place.
9	1974	The Amateur Athletic Union of the United States recognizes Tae Kwon Do as an official sport and elects Dr. Ken Min as the AAU Tae Kwon Do Committee's first national chairman.
10	1976	Tae Kwon Do is recognized by both the International Military Sports Council and the General assembly of International Sports Federation and becomes a world sport.
11	1979	The World Tae Kwon Do Federation is recognized by the International Olympic Committee (IOC).
12	1980	The World Tae Kwon Do Federation is granted recognition by the International Olympic Committee (IOC) at its 83rd General Session in Moscow.
13	1988	Tae Kwon Do is introduced as an exhibition game in the Seoul Olympic games.
14	2000	Tae Kwon Do is elected as an official sport at the 2000 Sydney Olympic games.

Japanese military did not destroy the spirit of the Korean people. Korean martial arts were revived following the restoration of Korea's independence. Many Korean martial art schools known as "Kwans" were opened, the main ones being Chung Do Kwan, Mooduk Kwan, Yun Moo Kwan, Chang Moo Kwan, Oh Do Kwan, Ji Do Kwan, Chi Do Kwan, and Sang Mu Kwan.

During the Korean War (1950–53) Syngman Rhee, the first president of the Republic of Korea (North), watched a demonstration of Korean martial arts masters led by Song Duk-Ki, a master of Taekkyon. Syngman Rhee was so impressed that he ordered that the training become a regular part of military training. Similarly, the South Vietnamese government requested instructors to train its troops in Tae Kwon Do during the Vietnam War.

On April 11, 1955, the various Kwans were united in a meeting among the masters. The majority of the Kwan masters agreed upon the name of Tae Soo Do. Two years later the name was changed to General Choi's suggestion of Tae Kwon Do. This name was chosen because it accurately describes the art, and it is similar to the art's early name of Taek Kyon. Following the foundation of the Korea Tae Kwon Do Association in 1961, many instructors were sent to demonstrate Tae Kwon Do throughout the world. The World Tae Kwon Do Federation (WTF) now coordinates Tae Kwon Do internationally.

Other martial arts styles

These days, there is a bewildering number of martial arts styles that people practice. Here is a quick glance at some of them so that we can determine what the differences are. It is good to have an idea of where Tae Kwon Do lies in the martial arts spectrum.

Karate

The style of martial art that most closely resembles Tae Kwon Do is Karate. It makes similar use of strikes, kicks, blocks, and punches. Indeed, the two styles have been an influence on each other through their development. The Japanese occupation of Korea affected Tae Kwon Do, but it was not all one-way traffic. The Karate style Koyokushinkai was actually founded by a Korean who lived in Japan.

Gichin Funakoshi (1868–1957) founded the style now known as Karate. Funakoshi was from the Japanese island of Okinawa, which is located close to both Korea and Japan. As a young man, Funakoshi learned the local indigenous style of martial art called "Tode" or "Chinese hand." He founded his own "Dojang" or training school where he taught his own interpretation of the art, which he called "Karate Do," or "the way of the empty hand."

Funakoshi went to the Japanese mainland in 1917 to demonstrate his new style to Crown Prince Hirohito. In 1922 his friend and sponsor, Jigoro Kano (the founder of Judo) invited Funakoshi to teach Karate at his Dojo.

Karate therefore gained a foothold in Japan and spread throughout the country. Many of Funakoshi's students founded their own styles of Karate, Wado Ryu being one of these.

The main difference between Karate and Tae Kwon Do is the greater emphasis that Tae Kwon Do has on kicking, although this difference can be misleading because some Karate instructors use a lot of kicks and some Tae Kwon Do instructors do not emphasize the kicking aspect as highly.

The real difference between the two is the way that the movements are expressed and the approach toward doing the movements. This difference is difficult to define in words but easy to see if you watch both styles.

Ju-jitsu

Ju-jitsu is another Japanese martial art. The literal translation is that "ju" means soft, and "jitsu" in this sense means art. So Ju-Jitsu means "the art of softness." This does not mean that Ju-jitsu people are soft! Soft in this sense means that you yield to an attack. Instead of trying to knock an attack out of the way, you yield to it and redirect it.

Ju-jitsu was the martial art of the samurai, and as such it is the elder brother of the other Japanese martial arts. Japanese martial arts take on the code of honor and philosophy adopted from the samurai.

Imagine a samurai warrior in battle. It is possible that he may become separated from his sword, but he must go on fighting, otherwise he will die. Ju-jitsu was the samurai's form of unarmed combat, and for this reason, many of the traditional Ju-jitsu techniques are designed to defeat an opponent swiftly and efficiently.

Ju-jitsu includes just about everything from the unarmed combat repertoire. It has kicks, blocks, strikes, and punches. It also contains many of the throws, locks, and strangleholds that are used in Judo. The difference is that many of the techniques of Ju-jitsu, such as neck locks, would not be safe to use on the Judo mat.

Ju-jitsu has a very wide scope. Different masters emphasized different areas for the training. Some masters would use harder techniques, while others would use soft, circular techniques. There could be an emphasis on strikes or an emphasis on locks. For this reason, there are several different styles of ju-jitsu around the world.

Judo

Judo has its roots in Ju-jitsu. In the 19th century, Ju-jitsu gained a somewhat undesirable reputation, as the wrong people were doing it and using it for the wrong reasons.

Jigoro Kano was a successful Ju-jitsu student of the time. He had studied the art in many of the best Japanese schools and had a good understanding of it. He saw that people behaving in an irresponsible way could easily destroy the art he loved. So Jigoro Kano set out to remove the most destructive techniques from the Ju-jitsu routines and make the martial art a safe and challenging training routine for the mind and body. The new system was named Judo.

Judo translates as "gentle way." The philosophy of the movement is to use your opponent's energy against him or her, and it is therefore a very efficient style of martial art.

All of the kicks, strikes, and dangerous locks were removed from the Ju-jitsu routine to create the Judo system. The new Judo system was now suitable for tournaments and competition.

Judo is a sophisticated wrestling style that incorporates the honor, philosophy, and respect of the martial arts. It is easily recognizable from the throws and groundwork that it incorporates.

It is a very popular martial art and is a popular Olympic event that is watched by millions worldwide. Judo attracts students or all ages, sizes, and abilities throughout the world.

Aikido

Aikido is a Japanese martial art founded by Morihei Ueshiba (1883–1966). Ueshiba studied under a martial art master called Takeda from 1912 until 1919, and he learned a variety of techniques that had been formalized by the Aizu clan. The style was called daito ryu-aiki Ju-jutsu. It is possible to trace this style back to the 6th century.

After studying with Takeda for seven years, Ueshiba devoted the next six years of his life to studying a spiritual tradition under Onisaburo Deguchi. He traveled throughout Asia with Deguchi working with the discipline.

In 1927, Ueshiba started a Dojang in Tokyo, teaching a mixture of the martial arts traditions that he had learned from Takeda and the spiritual tradition that he learned from Deguchi.

He eventually called this new style of teaching martial arts Aikido. The "Ai" means harmony, the "Ki" stands for the universal life force, and "Do" is the way. "Aikido" therefore translates as "the way of harmonizing spirit."

In Aikido, you harmonize with an attack. You do not try to deflect an attack; you draw it in toward you and neutralize it by redirecting it into a throw, joint lock, or other technique.

Aikido is classified as a soft style because it uses soft, circular blocking in a similar way to Tai Chi.

The Aikido student will not usually enter contests, as there are no competitions in traditional Aikido. This is in fitting with Ueshiba's idea that Aikido is not learning how to defeat others but learning how to defeat the negative characteristics that lie within all of us.

Hap Ki Do

Hap Ki Do means the "way of coordination and internal power." It is another Korean style.

Master Yong-Sul Choi (1904–86) founded modern Hap Ki Do in 1963. Like Tae Kwon Do, although it was founded relatively recently as a style, its roots go way back in Korean history to the Hwang Ra Do.

Hap Ki Do resembles Ju-jitsu or Aikido more than its Korean cousin, Tae Kwon Do. The reason for this is that the founder, Master Choi, studied under the Japanese master Takeda for many years. Takeda was also the instructor for Morihei Ueshiba, the founder of Aikido. It is therefore not surprising that Hap Ki Do has elements of the Ju-jitsu style from Takeda and the Aikido style from Ueshiba.

Yet Hap-Ki Do is a Korean style. It adopts the Korean style of attacking and has a greater emphasis on kicks than its Japanese cousins. This is a result of Master Choi's Korean influence on his new style.

Hap Ki Do is generally less common than Tae Kwon Do but still has a wide network of students, coaches, and masters throughout the world.

The Japanese martial art of Aikido is often taught as a self-defense technique.

Tai Chi

Tai Chi is a Chinese martial art that has been around in different forms since at least the 13th century. In the 17th century, much of the knowledge was formalized by the Chen family. In the 19th century, Yang Lu Chan founded another style from the Chen style. Yang Lu Chan's "Yang" style Tai Chi was popularized by his grandson Yang Chen Fu in the early 20th century.

Tai Chi and Aikido use very similar techniques that are executed in a slightly different way. The main rationale behind both is the concept of Yin and Yang. This idea has it that you use the interplay of opposites. If a hard force is coming toward you, the defense is to become soft and yield. This makes the attacker overextend his or her body so that you can control the attacker.

Tae Kwon Do is classified as a "hard" style, rather than a soft style like Tai Chi. The reason for this is the emphasis on powerful strikes and kicks, rather than the deflections and circular movement that Tai Chi uses.

Tai Chi is characterized by slow, graceful movements performed in a meditative manner.

Chapter 2   The philosophy of Tae Kwon Do

Spiritual philosophies such as Taoism were vital to the inception of Tae Kwon Do. Although much of Tae Kwon Do training is based on traditional methods, nothing remains static, and Tae Kwon Do continues to develop as further knowledge becomes integrated into the art.

To fully understand Tae Kwon Do, it is necessary to examine traditional Korean philosophy that has led to the development of Tae Kwon Do. The philosophy known as Hongik-ingan describes actions that benefit the universal welfare of mankind. Jaese-ihwa, a philosophy that means "divine rationalization of human beings," became part of the Hongik-ingan philosophy during the Old Chosun Age. Hongik-ingan philosophy was represented by Seon philosophy in the Koguryo period. The Seon philosophy included ideals such as national pride and "no retreat from fighting." The Seon philosophy was incorporated into martial arts training and was reflected in the Hwarangdo spirit during the Silla dynasty.

During the Silla kingdom period, a book known as the *Sesokokye* was published; it explained three characteristics of the Hwarangdo spirit. These characteristics were loyalty to your nation (Chung), filial piety to parents (Hyo), and trust (Shin). From these virtues the five principles of the world (Sye-Sok-Oh-Kye) and three virtuous conducts, or three kinds of beauty (Sam-mi), were formulated.

This philosophy became a basic way of life for the Hwarang, giving values and principles for living to those involved in martial art training. Tae Kwon Do spirit was inherited from the Hwarangdo spirit. This is evident from the five precepts of Tae Kwon Do, which are etiquette, perseverance, modesty, self-control, and indomitable spirit.

Korean temples incorporate details rarely seen in other Far Eastern temples, such as heavy tile roofs. (Mark Pawlett)

The five basic precepts of Tae Kwon Do and the qualities that they represent are as follows:

Etiquette (Ye Ui): to respect your instructors and your fellow students; to respect the grade that the person had attained; to be polite; to respect everyone as an individual.

Modesty (Yom Chi): to have the ability to remove the ego and believe that you are equal to all other humans, irrespective of their background or experience. This especially applies to instructors and competition winners.

Perseverance (In Nae): with patience you will achieve your goals.

Self-control (Guk Gi): this includes self-control when sparring as well as self-control in your everyday life.

Indomitable spirit (Baekjool Boolgool): to show courage when faced with a seemingly impossible situation; the ability to retain your fighting spirit.

Philosophy of the Hwarang – the sye-sok-oh-kye

1	sa-kun-lee-chung	loyalty to your country
2	sa-chin-lee-hyo	honor and respect your parents
3	kyo-u-lee-shin	trust and sincerity in friendship
4	lim-cheon-mu-t'wi	never to withdraw on the battlefield
5	sal-saeng-yu-taek	justice, not to take another life without just cause

the sam-mi

1	modesty	modesty refers to the spirit of contributing to social development, rather than that of the self.
2	frugality	frugality means not to waste
3	kyo-u-lee-shin	restraint

Tao

Taoism is an important part of Tae Kwon Do philosophy. It is very useful to have a grasp of the basic concepts of Taoism to fully understand the history and techniques used in Tae Kwon Do.

Taoism is regarded as a Chinese concept, although the ideas of Taoism are ancient and spread throughout the Far East. It was common for intellectuals in the Far East to have read the "Chinese Classics." This means, among other things, that they will have studied Taoism.

An understanding of Taoism helps you to understand the context within which the arts were invented and is a way of learning about another culture and way of life that can enrich your own lifestyle.

If you take a look at the Korean flag (below), you will instantly understand the emphasis and pride that the Koreans take in their Taoist spirituality. The symbol in the middle is the Yin-Yang symbol, and the bars around the outside are trigrams from the Chinese oracle, known as the I-Ching.

The first thing to understand is that Taoism is not a religion. Concepts such as the oneness of the universe are contemplated within Taoism, but no deity is worshiped, and there is no belief in a supernatural power that governs the universe.

Taoism comes from the observation of one's self in the universe and the interactions between the self and the universe. It is not as complicated as it sounds. For example, the seasons have an effect on us. When winter changes to spring, we feel changes inside ourselves. Without prejudging whether it is good or bad, Taoists will notice these changes. Understanding how you are in the world that you live in gives you the chance to feel a part of it, rather than exist as a lone entity that is buffeted by seemingly chaotic forces.

Taoism is not a thing that can be handed over to another person. It is based on exercises in experience, rather than an intellectual exercise. After work and study, you gradually start to learn and integrate the concepts and theories.

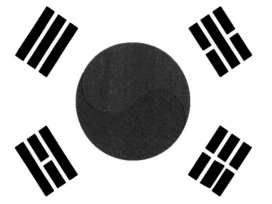

Yin and Yang

The concept of Yin and Yang are worth studying by the serious martial artist—no matter what his or her style.

The symbol is a very clever piece of graphic design. Look at it for a while and think about what it may be telling you.

Let's start by looking at the colors, black and white. Black represents Yin and white represents Yang. The color black is black because it absorbs light. Conversely the color white reflects all frequencies of light and looks white to the eye.

In Yin and Yang theory, Yin is the receptive (it absorbs) and Yang is the creative (it expands). The reflective white light represents the expansion of Yang, and the contraction of Yin is represented by the absorption of black.

So opposites can be described as being linked in pairs, such as life/death, hot/cold, up/down, in/out, etc.

This leads us to the idea that one cannot exist without the other. How can you have everything in one color—you would not need two or more colors because everything would be either black or white! The intermeshing of the two colors on the symbol represents this concept.

The circular shape of the symbol suggests that the coexistence between the entities of Yin and Yang is cyclic. Yin must follow the extreme of Yang, just as Yang must follow the extreme of Yin. A good example of this is breathing. After breathing in (Yin), the energy becomes Yang and you must breathe out.

There are many other concepts bound to the symbol, but the last one that we will discuss here is the dots in the halves of the symbol. This means that within Yin there is Yang, and within Yang there is Yin. An implication here is that Yin and Yang are not absolute; they are relative to each other.

If I have a flashlight that is brighter than yours, it gives out more energy, so it has more Yang energy. If the sun comes out, then it has much more energy than my feeble flashlight, so

my flashlight becomes Yin. But it is still Yang compared to your less bright one.

How does this apply to martial arts? The more you think about it, the more you will find, but here are a few examples based on what we have already discussed.

If you throw out your fist, it is a Yang movement because it is expanding or moving away from your body. If you pull your hand back for a block, then the movement is coming toward you and is Yin.

Now push your fist outward in a Yang move. Repeat the movement.

To repeat the movement, you needed to pull your hand back before you could push it out again. In Yin and Yang terms, you used the Yang energy when you pushed your fist out the first time, so you could not expand out with another fist until you had contracted and become more Yin first. It would be like trying to breathe out twice in a row.

This is true in all martial arts—if you try to stay expanded or contracted all of the time, you will not be able to move. Yin and Yang must therefore cycle.

Yang motion

Yin motion

The punch with the right hand is a Yang motion, while the left hand is in a protective Yin position.

I-Ching

In Taoism, there are no absolutes in Yin and Yang. If Yang becomes extreme, it gradually becomes Yin.

This idea gives rise to a view of the universe that can be described as a binary pattern of Yin and Yang combinations. This is the basic idea behind the I-Ching or *Book of Changes*.

The theory of the I-Ching is connected to the Taoist idea of creation. From the original source Wu Chi come the two opposites: Yin and Yang.

Yin and Yang are represented by a solid line or a broken line:

yang   **yin**

This kind of binary representation has resonances with modern computer technology. Just as a binary word on a computer is made of an array of binary digits, the characters of the I-Ching are made in the same way.

If we add another line to the original, we will have four different possibilities or combinations.

The addition of another line gives us three lines, and the three lines are commonly called "trigrams." Adding another binary digit to the system will give us eight possibilities, or eight characters. Each trigram is given different qualities, such as heaven, earth, thunder, etc. The attributes are based on the balance of Yin and Yang within the trigram. This is the fundamental building block for the I-Ching and will shortly be discussed in greater detail.

Grouping the trigrams together gives 8 x 8 = 64 possibilities. There are therefore 64 different hexagrams in the I-Ching or *Book of Changes*.

Ki

According to the philosophies of the East, there is an energy field that transforms our bodies from being empty vessels to a living entity. The Koreans and Japanese call this energy field "Ki," the Chinese call it "Chi," and Indian Yogis call it "Prana."

It is this same energy that a Shiatsu (energy massage) practitioner or an acupuncturist will use to try to heal a patient or client. The theory states that if the Ki in your body can flow evenly throughout your body, then you will be healthy. If the Ki becomes blocked or cannot flow for some reason, then illness can set in.

The less well-known Korean method of using energy to heal is called "Amma." It uses concepts from China and Japan and interprets them in a Korean way.

This kind of therapist will use touch to try to distribute the flow of Ki evenly. The acupuncturist will do the same with needles. Both techniques have become very popular in the West in recent years.

Healing and martial arts have been linked for many years because of this connection to Ki. Many of the great masters also had a good understanding of energetic healing or at least an instinctive feel for the subject.

The reason for this is that Ki can be channeled and put to different uses. If you want to use it to heal, then your mind will be in a very different thought pattern than if you wanted to hurt someone. In both instances, you will have projected your Ki, but the intention of your mind rules the way that it works.

If you want a demonstration of Ki, think about the Tae Kwon Do student who breaks pieces of wood with his strikes. If you are hitting a piece of wood, you do not aim at the piece of wood, you aim *through* it.

If you aim at the wood, you hurt your hand. If you aim through the wood, it breaks. This is an example of using your intent to extend the Ki. If you can develop sensitivity to Ki, then your Tae Kwon Do will change.

Danjon

In traditional Korean medicine, the Danjon is the name for the center of your abdominal region. This is the area just below your navel. In traditional Chinese medicine, it is called the Tan Tien, and the Japanese name for the whole abdominal area is the Hara.

In terms of Tae Kwon Do, our Danjon is the point through which all movement emanates. If you try to kick or punch using only an arm or leg, then your kicks and punches will be weak. If you can connect the movement to your Danjon, then you will use the whole of your body and the technique will be powerful.

In Korean thought, the Danjon is one of the most important energy centers in the human body. Those who are trained to be sensitive in such things can use the Danjon as a diagnostic area and can deduce physical or emotional problems in a person by touching or examining the Danjon area

The therapist assesses and senses the Ki of a person in the Danjon where all the different energies in the body meet. By touching a specific area, it is possible to determine the state of those energies.

Your Danjon is like a second brain. We already know this in a way, and it is reflected in our language: we have all had a "gut reaction" to a situation.

Practicing meditations like the one described later (see page 100) will increase your sense of your Danjon, and your "second brain" in the Danjon will communicate better. This is really a non-intellectual type of communication, but it is also very intuitive.

We all know what it is like when trying to use logic to decide what to do in a situation. We weigh up the pros and cons and then usually decide to go with what our "gut reaction" told us in the first place.

If you can develop your sense of Danjon, you can sidestep the weighing up part and go straight for the action

In a fighting situation, this means that you will be able to react without having to weigh up the process in your thinking mind. This will make you much faster and more accurate—both useful tricks for Tae Kwon Do!

Chapter 3   Is it for me?

Is Tae Kwon Do suitable for you? If you want to do it, then yes, it is. All you need is the motivation to begin, and the driving force behind that motivation will vary from person to person.

The Tae Kwon Do student will benefit from increased physical fitness and psychological well-being. Physically, the student will improve stamina, strength, flexibility, balance, and control. Psychologically, Tae Kwon Do is known to reduce tension, depression, anger, fatigue, and confusion and to increase mental vigor in both male and female participants (Toscovic, 2001). Additionally, Tae Kwon Do has been shown to improve leadership skills (Kurian, 1993).

There is no real minimum age that a student can begin studying Tae Kwon Do. Tae Kwon Do can be an ideal sport for children as it can teach them discipline and self-confidence, backed up with fitness training.

Some of the harder stretches and conditioning exercises (such as knuckle push ups) should be left until you are older.

There are no age limits in Tae Kwon Do. Older people should speak to their doctor to assess their fitness before starting Tae Kwon Do. There are very few medical conditions that completely exclude you from training. If you can devise a plan between your instructor and your doctor, you should be OK. Recent research (Brudnak et al., 2001) shows that through Tae Kwon Do, elderly students can increase the number of push ups, trunk flexion, and balance time on each foot. The presence of older people in a club is often positive, as their maturity may influence some of the younger students.

What do I need?

When you first enter the Dojang or training hall, most instructors will allow the student to train in sweatpants and a T-shirt. Tae Kwon Do is usually done barefoot, so this saves on the cost of footwear!

When you have decided if Tae Kwon Do is for you, then you will be expected to buy a "dobok." The dobok is the traditional outfit for training in many martial arts. The Tae Kwon Do dobok tends to be made from a lighter material than Judo Gi's because they are less likely to get torn. The basic dobok will usually start at around $30–$40.

After a while, your instructor will start to teach you "kyorugi" or sparring. If you intend to practice sparring, it is sensible to invest in protective equipment. Try to buy the best quality that you can afford, as it works better and lasts longer.

There are many types of body armor and head protectors available. Some Tae Kwon Do associations do not use any at all, and your instructor will advise you if you need to buy them. If it is essential, the club will usually have items to borrow.

Your club will usually possess such items as kicking paddles, focus mitts, body armor, and head protection, although there is nothing to stop you from buying your own if you really "get the bug."

1	**Gum shield (white or translucent)**	Costs a lot less than getting your teeth fixed. Buy a good one that will not slip out of your mouth. Consult your dentist if in doubt about the quality.
2	**Groin protector**	Well, we don't really need to say much about that! Buy a proper martial arts groin protector, not the "football" type, as it will give better protection. Women should not forget this equipment either. The further it extends into your abdominal region without limiting your movement, the better.
3	**Bust protector**	Obviously for women.
4	**Head guard**	Protects the sides and top of the head.
5	**Body protector or hogu**	Protects the chest and stomach.
6	**Forearm protector**	Prevents bruises to the forearm.
7	**Shin protector**	Shin bruises are very common Tae Kwon Do injuries.

Belts and grades

When you go to your first Tae Kwon Do class, you will see the Tae Kwon Do students arranged in neat lines. The ones at the front will have black belts and those at the back, white belts. Students in the middle will have various colored belts.

The color of the belts will tell you the level of training that the Tae Kwon Do student has reached through his or her gradings.

The belts are in a hierarchical sequence that always starts with white belt and finishes with black belt. The intermediate belts represent the grade of intermediate Tae Kwon Do students.

Shown here are the belt colors from white to black for Tae Kwon Do.

Attaining the grade of black belt is a great achievement in Tae Kwon Do.

level	grade	
10th Kup		white
9th Kup		yellow tag on white belt
8th Kup		yellow belt
7th Kup		yellow belt with green tag
6th Kup		green belt
5th Kup		green belt with blue tag
4th Kup		blue belt
3rd Kup		blue belt with red tag
2nd Kup		red
1st Kup		red with black tag
1st Dan		black

The word "Kup" means grades away from the black belt (Dan). The 8th Kup, for example, means that the Tae Kwon Do student has eight more full gradings before he or she reaches the coveted black belt.

When you reach black belt, it does not stop there! Many say that it has just started. There are various levels of black belt, called "Dan grades," starting at 1st Dan and progressing to 10th Dan. A stripe on the end of the black belt sometimes denotes the level of the black belt.

The skill level of the Tae Kwon Do movements required for gradings depend on the grade of the student. In gradings you will be required to perform the last poomsae that you have learned, and possibly some previous ones. Movements applicable to the skill level of the student will be inspected. The 10th Kup is not expected to show any kyorugi (or sparring). Higher Kup grades will be required to perform kyorugi.

The Tae Kwon Do class

It is impossible to learn any martial arts by theory alone. Without practice, it amounts to nothing more than intellectual play. So, you have decided to try Tae Kwon Do. What next?

Well, here you have two options. You could either try to learn from books like this one and take years to learn the technique in a very limited manner, or forget that idea and join a class.

It is probably best to choose the "join a class" option. We will take a look later at ways of determining what sort of class you are joining, but for now, let's consider what happens when you go to the class.

Normally, it is best to contact the instructor before you arrive. Many instructors do not demand this, but it gives them a chance to meet you for a few minutes before the class starts. The instructor will normally talk about about any specific needs, medical or non-medical, that you may have. It also gives you the chance to get to know your instructor.

The next stage depends upon the instructor. Some will ask you to watch for a while so that you can decide before you take the plunge. It is more common these days for the new Tae Kwon Do student just to join in with the beginners. Sometimes a higher-graded student will teach you the basics, such as Dojang etiquette (see page 48).

The class will always start with warm-up exercises. This will be followed by a mixture of Tae Kwon Do movements such as kicking, blocking and hand strikes, patterns (poomsae), self-defense, sparring techniques, and sparring.

The ratios of these will usually vary, depending upon the club and what the instructor wants to work on for that lesson. Additionally, various stretches are usually performed during the class.

We will analyze the three physical training areas—the basics, patterns, and sparring—throughout this book.

Many advanced Tae Kwon Do techniques are rooted in the basic maneuvers.

Choosing a club

Martial arts are more popular now than they have ever been. We come from a small market town in England. Back in the 1980s, the only choice in this town was Tae Kwon Do. Twenty years later, there are now at least ten martial arts clubs to choose from. If you visit a city like London, you will almost be able to have a separate telephone directory just for the martial arts clubs.

This can be a very healthy thing. It means that the potential martial arts student does not have to stick to the one and only club that it is practical for him or her to get to. The flipside of this argument is that quantity does not always bring quality.

So, you have found a club that is within a reasonable traveling distance. The instructor sounds OK on the phone, but how can you tell if it is a good club? Well, the truth is that there is not really a test that will tell you for certain. It could be that an instructor who has something good to offer does not meet many of the normal guidelines. Also, what suits one student will not always suit another.

Instructors should follow and teach the precepts of etiquette, modesty, perseverance, and indomitable spirit.

Having said that, there are a few things to look out for. Here is a list of them:

1	The instructor	Is the instructor the type of person whom you feel you can learn from? Can you speak with the instructor openly? Is the instructor qualified to teach the style?
2	The senior students	If you join the club, you will be following what the senior students have done. Is that what you want? Take the opportunity to talk to them, swap a few stories, and get the measure of where they are with their training. Is it what you want to do? Do not forget that much of your learning, in the early days at least, will be from the senior students.
3	Attitude to injury	Some teachers can be very cavalier in their attitude toward injury. Mention the subject and check that the instructor is saying the kind of things that you want to hear.

4	Insurance	Most martial arts clubs these days will offer some kind of insurance against any possible injury. With some of the softer styles like Tai Chi, it is not really needed, as there is little or no contact. In Tae Kwon Do you will be sparring and practicing dangerous techniques. It is essential to have insurance against mistakes.
5	Affiliation	If an instructor is affiliated with some board or body, then he or she will have had to make the grade to become affiliated. This is a good quality benchmark. There is nothing to stop anybody from setting up a martial arts club. To keep a check on the quality of instruction, many martial arts associations will issue a list of instructors. Your instructor should be on such a list because this will prove that he or she has the skills to teach you the style. The two biggest Tae Kwon Do federations are the World Tae Kwon Do Federation (WTF) and the International Tae Kwon Do Federation (ITF). Be sure to ask questions if your club is not affiliated with one of these organizations.

Type of Tae Kwon Do club

In reality, most people take a look at the nearest club to them, and if it fits, they stick with it. This is good up to a point, but locality should not be the only factor in your decision. Have a look at some of the other styles and see how they compare. Try to get the flavor of the different styles, as it will improve your overall understanding of Tae Kwon Do. Really, the choice between the styles is one of taste—if you like it, it is good.

Sport Tae Kwon Do or traditional Tae Kwon Do

Most of this book is really dedicated to traditional Tae Kwon Do. In traditional Tae Kwon Do, you will learn the whole scope of Tae Kwon Do including the basics, poomsae, sparring, and the philosophy behind it.

Sport Tae Kwon Do is a kind of specialization where the Tae Kwon Do student will concentrate mainly on the sparring aspect of Tae Kwon Do. Students of these clubs will concentrate very hard on their sparring and fitness for sparring. The aim will usually be to enter sparring competitions and, hopefully, win them.

Both traditional Tae Kwon Do and sport Tae Kwon Do are important parts of Tae Kwon Do. Think about the emphasis that you want from your training and inform your instructor so that he or she knows what you intend to achieve.

A good Tae Kwon Do club should teach both traditional (see opposite page) and the modern sport of Tae Kwon Do.

Dojang etiquette

When you enter or leave a Tae Kwon Do Dojang, you should always bow. It does not matter whether it is a purpose-built Dojang or the local village hall—for the Tae Kwon Do lesson, it is all the same thing. Even if you just have to make a

Etiquette is an important aspect of Tae Kwon Do philosophy and should continue in everyday life.

visit to the bathroom, you should always bow on the way out and on the way back in.

At the beginning and end of your class, you will perform the standing bow to the instructor. Before training with a partner, you should bow. When you have finished training with that partner, you should bow again. If you are going to train with another partner, you should do the same.

The bow is a sign of respect. When you enter or leave the Dojang, it is a sign that you have respect for the Dojang. When you bow to the instructor, you are not bowing to show sub-servience to the person in front of you. You are bowing to show respect for the person, what he or she has done in the pursuit of Tae Kwon Do knowledge, and all that has gone before him.

When you bow to your training partner, you are showing your partner respect and gratitude for the chance to train with that person, whoever he or she is.

With the bow, there should be a sense of openness and respect. It has nothing at all to do with your ego or the ego of the person that you are bowing to. If you subtract the respect element from martial arts, you remove one of the most valuable lessons that martial arts have to teach, both to individuals and to the world at large!

Other general rules include: do not eat or smoke in the Dojang; keep your Dobok clean and wear it properly; and always respect the instructor and fellow students without prejudice.

The bow (kunyeh)

The bow should always be done with a sense of respect and humility—never just for the sake of it.

1. At ease—shui.

2. Move your heels together into the attention stance (charyot seogi) with the arms flat at the sides, body upright, and the head held high.

3. Bend from the hips to an angle of around 30 degrees.

4. After one second in the bowing position, straighten the body back into the attention position.

5. Jumbi seogi.

Chapter 4 Fitness for Tae Kwon Do

People learn Tae Kwon Do for many reasons, one of which is fitness. After training for a while, students often realize that Tae Kwon Do is much more than just a physical fitness system.

Frequent training is the best way to improve fitness. Try to practice for an extra two hours a week, in addition to your Tae Kwon Do lessons. Split this time into several short sessions, rather than one long workout at the end of the week.

Fitness has many different aspects, depending upon the aims of the individual, and can encompass mind, body, or even spiritual fitness. Initially, you need to define your aims, which may change from time to time. In the beginning, you may get out of breath while sparring. This suggests that you need to work on your cardiovascular training.

After this hurdle, you may need to improve your power or suppleness. You may also find that you cannot focus your mind when performing poomsae, so meditation may help in this instance. Experiment and find out. Make your learning your own!

The exercises shown here are designed so that you can practice them at home. Try to vary your routine. Include other exercises that you may have learned.

If you do the same exercises all the time, your body becomes accustomed to them, so development may be slow. If you can vary your routine from day to day, progress will be faster and less boring.

These exercises are, in general, quite simple. If you are

unsure about anything, ask your instructor—confusion can can result in injury. Also, take it easy! Tae Kwon Do is for life—you have all the time that you need, so don't rush.

Think about it like this: if you went to the gymnasium and saw a person lift 600 pounds (300 kilograms), you would be impressed. It would not be sensible for a beginner to try to copy him or her. The exercises described here are similar. If you cannot do a certain stretch, do not force yourself. Allow your body to gradually change, and you will avoid injury.

Remember, if you injure yourself by trying to do too much too fast, you will not be able to train.

Flexibility is an important aspect of Tae Kwon Do training.

Diet and nutrition

Do you think that it is possible to be a Tae Kwon Do champion if your diet consists mainly of pizza and soft drinks? No, it would not make sense, would it?

If you are serious about your fitness, you also need to think about your diet. You need to consider not only the food you eat, but also what you drink, and any other habits that you may have.

The range of different ideas about diet is bewildering. This is partly because the human body is a very complex system. Many people have worked out different approaches, some good and some bad, and of course, there is frequently a fashion element to a diet.

If diet is something that interests you, there are many good books and courses available. Take a look in your local library to get some idea, and assess your own needs, not what the latest fashions are!

The basic rule for any diet is that you will lose body fat if you simply eat fewer calories than you burn. The key is to maintain a balanced diet so that your body can function healthily. This involves eating all the basic nutrients that the body needs and avoiding overeating. To maintain muscle mass, you should aim to lose no more than one to two pounds per week. Rather than dieting, think of making permanent lifestyle changes. Simply sticking to a calorie-restricted diet for a number of days or weeks probably won't give you permanent results. Focus on weight management instead of weight loss.

In martial arts and healing arts, there is an idea of being "grounded." The White Rabbit from *Alice in Wonderland*, who rushed from place to place virtually without stopping, never pausing to consider the present, was the opposite of grounded. To be grounded means that you have a good sense of the present moment. As you can imagine, being grounded is a useful quality for a martial artist.

The food you eat can affect your sense of grounding. For example, if you drink too much coffee or other caffeinated drinks, it can make you feel edgy. Other examples are alcohol, and food with a large amount of preservatives or added chemicals. Natural, pure food that has not been tampered with too much is healthier.

Apart from the more esoteric aspects of food energetics such as grounding, there are also scientific facts that are useful to know about food and nutrition.

A healthy diet with plenty of fresh food will help improve fitness levels.

Food as fuel

Why do we need to eat? One reason is that food provides us with the energy that we need to survive, in the same way that a car needs fuel to run. The energy in food is measured in calories. Calories represent the amount of heat released when food is broken down in your body.

The two principal types of food that provide energy are:	
1	carbohydrate
2	fat

The ideal diet for sports such as Tae Kwon Do should be biased toward a high proportion of carbohydrate and a low proportion of fat, with sufficient supply of protein and fiber, as well as plenty of fluid.

The average Western diet tends toward the more fatty foods. It is worthwhile examining the food groups to gain a better understanding of our diets.

Carbohydrates

There are two kinds of carbohydrates. The first is the simple carbohydrate. Simple carbohydrates include things like cakes, sweets, sugar, chocolate, etc. These provide a quick energy boost and very little else. These also include foods like fruits and milk. Although some simple carbohydrates in the diet should be restricted, they can provide an energy boost when needed, for example, after a hard workout.

More useful are the complex carbohydrates such as potatoes, rice, vegetables, and pasta. These complex carbohydrates are released more slowly into your blood stream, and therefore enable your body to maintain a balanced blood sugar level. Complex carbohydrates also contain vital elements such as vitamins and minerals, and are high in fiber.

"Fast food" like this hamburger and fries tends to be full of saturated fats.

Fat

Fat contains more energy than carbohydrates, which is why we find it easy to eat too much fat. The human body can synthesize most fatty acids from the products of carbohydrate and protein metabolism. However, a few fatty acids, such as linoleic and linoleic acids, are termed essential fatty acids because the body cannot synthesize them, and so they must be supplied by the diet.

It should always be remembered that high-fat diets are now known to cause many chronic health problems such as heart disease and diabetes.

There are different types of fats, frequently categorized into saturated fat, polyunsaturated fat, and monounsaturated fat.

Polyunsaturated fats

Polyunsaturated fats can be classified into two types known as omega-3 and omega-6. Generally, people are deficient in the omega-3 fats, which are found in oily fish such as herring, mackerel, salmon, and sardines, and from walnuts, pumpkin seeds, and linseeds. Omega-3 fats benefit the human body as they are anti-inflammatory, protective, and speed up the metabolism. The essential fatty acids contained in omega-3 fats are alpha-linoleic acid, eicosapentaenoic acid, and docosahesxaenoic acid.

The omega-6 fatty acids are much more common in the modern diet and are found in food products such as corn, soybean, and sunflower oils. In general, omega-6 fatty acid consumption should be restricted. However, the omega fatty acids linoleic acid and gamma-linoleic acid are essential fatty acids and should be incorporated into the diet. Too much of the omega-6 fatty acids (with the exception of gamma-linoleic acid) can increase inflammation and suppress the immune function.

Certain processes, such as hydrogenation and frying, turn polyunsaturated fats into the more damaging trans fatty acids. Hydrogenation transforms oils into solids such as margarine. This process removes nutrients such as vitamin E, but gives the product a longer shelf life. Processing fresh oils in this way alters the chemical structure of the fats so that the relevant receptor sites within the body are unable to recognize and utilize them. In addition, they actually prevent the uptake of the essential fatty acids. Among the worst of the "bad" fats are margarine and the fats found in any fried food.

Saturated fat usually comes from animal products and tends to be more solid. They are also found in coconut oil, palm kernel oil, and vegetable lard. Very small amounts are required in a healthy diet. Saturated fats should not constitute of more than 10 percent of total calorie intake, as they can lead to heart disease and high cholesterol.

Monounsaturated fat is found in nuts and olive oil and is healthier than saturated fat, as it contains less cholesterol.

Omega-9 fatty acids are monounsaturated fats and can be synthesized by humans in a limited amount; they are also found in olive oil.

Cholesterol

Cholesterol is a fatty substance that is found in foods like egg yolks, butter, whole milk, meat, cheese, and cream. Our bodies need cholesterol and can usually produce the required quantity, in addition to what we consume.

Cholesterol is transported around the body by combining with lipoproteins (molecules that are a combination of lipids and proteins). Most of the cholesterol found in the body is found in the low density lipoproteins (LDLPs). LDLPs form deposits in arteries and may cause the formation of blood clots. High density lipoproteins (HDLPs) are not considered harmful.

Protein

Your body needs protein to repair and grow tissues like muscles, hair, and fingernails, among a variety of other vital functions. Protein can also provide a source of energy. Generally, the body uses carbohydrates and fat for energy, but when there is inadequate dietary fat or carbohydrates, then protein can be used.

Proteins are complex molecules comprised of linked amino acids. Amino acids are simple compounds containing carbon, hydrogen, oxygen, nitrogen, and sulphur. Proteins are broken down into amino acids during digestion, and the amino

acids are then absorbed into the body to produce new proteins.

The human body can produce some amino acids. However, the essential amino acids cannot be made, and so they must be supplied in the diet. The eight essential amino acids required by humans are leucine, isoleucine, valine, threonine, methionine, phenylalanine, tryptophan, and lysine.

Most people who eat moderate amounts of protein-rich food will have more protein than they need. As a guideline, the average healthy adult requires a minimum of 1 pound (0.45 kilograms) of protein for every 2 pounds (0.90 kilograms) of body mass. This can rise to 1 pound of protein for each pound of body mass for people who exercise regularly.

Foods that supply the most protein in a vegan diet are legumes (peas, beans, lentils, and soya products), grains (wheat, oats, rice, barley, buckwheat, millet, pasta, and bread), nuts (Brazils, hazels, almonds, and cashews) and seeds (sunflower, pumpkin, and sesame). Many plant proteins are low in one of the essential amino acids. For example, grains tend to be low in lysine, while legumes are low in methionine. Therefore, it is important for vegetarians to have a varied diet.

Be careful with red meat. Although it contains protein, it also contains saturated fats. White meat, vegetables, and fish provide less fatty sources of protein.

Meat and eggs are important sources of protein, although it is also present in legumes, grains, and nuts.

Vitamins and minerals

Vitamins and minerals are essential parts of your diet that your body cannot make by itself (the exceptions are niacin and vitamin D). They perform many vital functions in the body, and a balanced diet will provide the daily requirement of all vitamins and minerals. If your lifestyle causes you to miss the odd meal, vitamin supplements are better than missing out completely. However, it must be stressed that vitamin supplements are not a substitute for a balanced diet.

This dietary information is just a guideline to help you make informed decisions about diet. It

is worth reading around the subject of nutrition—many people tend to be more concerned about the fuel that they put into their vehicles rather than the food that they put into themselves.

There is one essential part of the diet, without which we would die and from which many people are suffering a deficiency in their bodies. If you have not guessed it yet, it is water.

Fresh vegetables and fruit are the best sources of vitamins and minerals vital to good health.

The following table is a brief summary of dietary
vitamins, their sources, and their benefits.

Vitamin	Benefits	Sources
A	Strong bones, eyesight, and healthy skin	Eggs, butter, oily fish, liver, kidneys
B1	Growth and converting blood sugar to energy	Seafood, beans, whole-grain foods, rice
B2	Production of energy and cell growth	Dairy foods, green vegetables, yeast, liver
B3	Nervous system, digestion, and sex hormones	Meat and fish, chicken, nuts, avocados
B5	Healing, fighting infection, and immune system	Whole-grain products, fish, eggs, chicken, nuts
B6	Nervous system and cell production	Meat, cabbage, melon, egg, whole grains
B12	Energy, nervous system, growth in children	Meat, fish, poultry, dairy, produce
C	Healthy bones, muscles, healing, and protection	Fruits and vegetables and potatoes
D	Absorption of calcium for teeth and bones	Dairy products such as milk and fish oils
E	Absorbing iron to protect the circulatory system	Whole-grain products, nuts, eggs, milk, avocados
K	Healthy blood clotting	Fruits and vegetables and potatoes

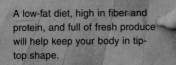

A low-fat diet, high in fiber and protein, and full of fresh produce will help keep your body in tip-top shape.

Water

It seems strange that so many people suffer from dehydration in the Western world, where there is an abundance of drinkable water, when people are dying of thirst in other parts of the world.

One reason for this is the popularity of drinks containing caffeine and alcohol, which are diuretics and make you urinate. Sugary drinks can also cause dehydration by drawing fluid toward the digestive system.

Our bodies are finely balanced as far as water is concerned. Dehydration alters cardiovascular, thermoregulatory, central nervous system, and metabolic functions. One or more of these alterations will degrade endurance exercise performance when dehydration exceeds 2 percent of body weight (Cheuvront et al., 2003). If you are already on the edge of dehydration from drinking coffee all day in a hot office, it will not take much sweating in your training session before dehydration makes its impact.

The obvious answer is to drink more water. To minimize the adverse effects of body water deficits on endurance exercise performance, it is recommended that fluid intake should be sufficient to minimize dehydration to less than 2 percent of body weight loss. This can usually be achieved with fluid intakes of less than 1 liter per hour. Water has many benefits: it maintains better mental and physical performance, and also helps in the removal of toxins and keeping your skin clear.

Thirst is not a reliable indicator. If you wait until you are thirsty, you are already dehydrated. Try to drink water regularly during the day, and if you have a long training session, try to have a small drink during your break, if you have one.

Steps toward improving your diet

Diet is very much a personal thing. We all have our own individual needs and desires. If you are already on a special diet, for whatever reason, it is not intended that this information conflict with the needs of that diet. The following advice is based on the sort of general suggestions that a personal trainer in a gymnasium, for example, might give. It assumes that there are no special needs or requirements, but it is not the whole story. For detailed nutritional information, you need to study the subject more thoroughly or consult an expert.

You may find the following steps useful:

1	Try to gain your energy from carbohydrates rather than fats	Dishes like rice, pasta, potatoes, and noodles are good sources of energy derived from complex carbohydrates. Fat has 9 calories per gram, whereas carbohydrates have 4 calories per gram. Therefore, it is much easier to restrict your calorific intake by restricting your fat.
2	Watch the fat!	Grill or boil food rather than frying it. Eat chicken, fish, or soya rather than red meat. When you do eat red meat, choose lean cuts and trim off the fat. Choose low-fat options when shopping for your food. Change from full-fat to half-fat milk. Instead of butter, use a spread high in polyunsaturated fats. Remove the skin before eating poultry, as this contains most of the fat.
3	Choose healthy snacks	Instead of a bag of chips and a bar of chocolate, try fruit (dried or fresh), nuts, raisins, rice cakes, or bread.
4	Drink plenty of water	Sometimes when your body craves water, the signal can be misinterpreted as hunger. Try drinking water throughout the day.
5	Eat regularly rather than large meals	Skipping meals can make you feel hungry for the rest of the day. Breakfast is especially important if you want to avoid the cravings for snacks during the day. Little and often is best for sustained energy levels.
6	Avoid eating too much late at night	If you eat late at night, it can affect the restful quality of your sleep. Indeed, some foods can disturb your system enough to cause bad dreams. Also, if you eat late at night, much of the energy cannot be used and will, therefore, be stored as fat. Your metabolic rate is much slower while sleeping, and so your body burns fewer calories. However, it is important not to miss out on meals. If you eat late, then choose low-calorie meals.
7	Restrict the salt content of your diet	Generally, you can consume enough salt in your diet without the need to add to it. Excessive salt consumption can lead to high blood pressure.
8	Eat plenty of fruits and vegetables	If you eat a varied diet with at least five portions of fresh fruit and vegetables every day, you are unlikely to lack any essential dietary requirement.

Warm-up exercises

The most common cause of injuries in Tae Kwon Do is the lack of a proper warm-up. If you are late to a class, it is tempting to run into the Dojang, get changed quickly, and start training. If this means that you miss out on your warm-up exercises, you are entering the risk category for injuries. For this reason, most instructors will force the student to do some warm-up exercises before he or she is permitted to train.

Similarly, it is important to warm up when you are training at home. It is beneficial to train in between lessons. If you do train at home, then you should go through some warm-up exercises, even if you are just going to do a little bit of stretching.

Warm-up exercises prepare the body and mind for the exercises to come and therefore protect you from injury.

Tae Kwon Do lessons start with gentle warm-up exercises and probably move through quite intense stretching and cardiovascular exercises. This means that during the lesson, your muscles will have become quite warm, making them ready for stretching. For this reason, it is a good idea to have a "warming-down" or "cooling-off" period after a heavy training session to aid the transition from the training environment to non-training.

For warming-down exercises, your coach will usually take you through some of the warm-up exercises, but done in a fairly gentle way.

We will now look through a series of exercises that are useful for warming up your body. These exercises are intended to get the joints moving. The exercises that you need to increase your cardiovascular movement are covered in a separate section.

Warm-up exercises: neck

If you do not know the feeling of getting a stiff neck, then you are lucky. A slight strain to the muscles in the neck can cause headaches, irritability, and sickness. Even worse, it can prevent you from training.

The following neck exercises are useful to include with your warm-up sequence or just for general body maintenance. Using the exercise when you get up in the morning or during the day can help you take care of your neck.

Neck exercise: left and right

This is a simple exercise that can be done either seated or standing.

Use your eyes and imagine that you are drawing a large circle with them, as you make a circle with your head. Repeat the exercise in both directions and remember to keep breathing steadily. At the high point, do not let your head just rock backward, as this can cause strain on the upper vertebrae.

Warm-up exercises: shoulders

Tae Kwon Do has many blocks, strikes, and punches using the arms. If your shoulders are as stiff as old lumps of wood, it is impossible for you to do these actions smoothly.

Shoulder exercise 1: rotations

If you do have neck problems, this exercise can be helpful, as it can reduce tension in the trapezius muscles in the back of the neck.

1. Inhale as you raise your shoulders in an upward arc.

2. Exhale as you lower the shoulders in a downward arc. Repeat in the other direction.

Shoulder exercise 2: windmill

This exercise can be done quickly or slowly. If you do it slowly, it is good to open the joints. Increasing the speed reduces the efficiency to open the joints but helps to get the blood pumping around your shoulder area.

1. To do the exercise, just swing your arm around in a circle. Try to do a similar amount of exercise in both directions with each arm.

2. If you want a more challenging exercise, try swinging one arm forward and one arm backward.

Warm-up exercises: waist

In Tae Kwon Do, the hips, waist, and abdominal area are the core of your movement. In traditional Korean Amma or Japanese Shiatsu medicine, the Danjon—the abdominal region—is the energetic center. If your range of motion in this area is limited, then the whole way that you move your body will be limited.

Waist exercise 1: rotation

Try to keep your body straight, so that the movement is in the waist and not your head bobbing up and down. One way of doing this is to focus your eyes on an object. If it looks like the object is moving, then ease off with the exercise until you are within a range of motion where you can keep your head still.

1. Start in a standing position. Put your hands on your kidneys. Push forward with your hands.

2. Rotate your body to the left or right. Repeat in the other direction.

Waist exercise 2: rotation

This exercise is fundamental to the way that martial arts work. If you can use your waist area to create a rotation that transmits through the arm, you will have a powerful strike.

1. Start in a standing position. Turn your waist to the left and right, keeping your arms relaxed.

2. As the momentum of your waist increases, your arms will swing further.

Warm-up exercises: knees

In Tae Kwon Do, you will be kicking. Stance work also requires strong and supple legs—these exercises can help.

Knee exercise 1: rotation

You will find that this exercise is excellent for loosening the hip joint and strengthening the thighs.

1. Start by lifting your knee high in front of your body.

2. Draw a circle with your knee in either direction. Count the number that you do in one direction and do the same in the other direction. Repeat with the other leg.

Knee exercise 2: rotation

If you have delicate knees, this exercise is prob-ably best avoided, as it is possible that it could aggravate the situation. If you feel any pain what-soever during the exercise, you should either ease off or stop completely.

1. Put your feet together, bend your knees, and place your hands on your knees. Focus your eyes on a point on the floor to aid your balance.

2. Rotate the knees, first in one direction and then the other. Do not overdo the rotation; it is really just to get some movement into the knees.

Warm-up exercises: ankles

Do not forget about your ankles. In stance work, your feet are your connection with the floor. If your ankles are stiff, then the vital connection between your body and the floor is reduced. It is also useful to have supple ankles for kicking.

Ankle exercise: rotation

This exercise is shown in the standing position, but there is nothing stopping you from doing the exercise while sitting at a desk. Nobody will see you doing it, and it can have an energetically grounding quality when used in this way.

Touch the floor with the ball of your foot. Make a rotation with your knee, and this will work the ankle.

Try the rotation in both directions. Work with both legs.

Stretching for Tae Kwon Do

Stretching has many benefits to the Tae Kwon Do student. One obvious benefit that follows from the warm-up exercises is the reduced risk of injury. The reduction in muscular tension and greater elasticity that stretching brings are factors that can reduce the risk of muscular injury or joint sprain.

Stretching has many other benefits. The increased range of motion will allow the Tae Kwon Do student to kick higher. In addition, the muscular relaxation that comes from stretching causes a mental relaxation. This kind of mental relaxation allows a greater body awareness that is vital for the diligent Tae Kwon Do student.

Stretching is only of benefit when done properly. Tae Kwon Do students must incorporate stretching into their daily routines if they want to see proper results. Stretches must be done slowly and gradually.

There are various approaches to stretching. Generally, painful exercises that actually damage the body have been replaced by more gentle stretching exercise routines. The most common methods of stretching can be described as static or dynamic.

1. Static stretching

Static stretching is designed to extend a joint through a wide range of motion. This is the kind of stretching often performed in Yoga classes. It involves stretching part of your body to your furthest point and holding the stretch. It is a very simple and safe method, but it must be balanced with strength training, otherwise you may lose some muscle performance.

Variations on static stretching include assisted stretching, ballistic stretching, and proprioceptive neuromuscular facilitation.

Assisted stretching

Assisted stretching is static stretching done with a training partner. In assisted stretching, you try to relax your body while an external force extends the stretch. A common example of this is where one Tae Kwon Do student helps the other to stretch the legs by pushing them out.

Assisted stretching is effective but can lead to muscular soreness and should be done slowly and with caution to prevent injury. The person being stretched must remain relaxed.

Ballistic stretching

In ballistic stretching the stretch position is maintained with repeated body movements. This is done by stretching similarly to static stretching but with bouncing at the end of the stretch. From a position of maximum stretch, ease off for a fraction of a second before bouncing into the stretch again.

This is a rather dangerous method because it does not give the muscle tissues time to adapt into the stretch. Such stretching may induce muscle tear if the stretch tolerance of the muscles is misjudged.

Different forms of lunge stretch.

Proprioceptive neuromuscular facilitation

Proprioceptors are spindles located in muscle. They provide the brain with information concerning the position of the limb, thereby enabling limb movements to be coordinated. Proprioceptors, known as the Golgi tendon organ, are located in muscles and joints. These protect muscles by telling them to relax when the muscle is under maximal tension.

At the extreme position of the stretch, the muscle is voluntarily tensed without any change in limb position (known as an isometric contraction). This isometric contraction further increases the tension in the tendons. The Golgi tendon organ becomes activated and causes the muscle to relax. This reflex is known as proprioceptive neuromuscular facilitation (PNF). This function protects the muscle from injury by stopping the muscle from stretching too far.

If the isometric contraction is then stopped, the muscle group being stretched will relax, thereby allowing the muscle to be stretched still further.

This sequence of stretch-tense-relax can be performed a number of times to increase your range during stretching. Such a stretch can be achieved if you have a partner to help you during stretching. For example, use a partner to push out your legs to help you get into the box splits (see assisted stretching). Maximally tense your muscles for about five or six seconds by trying to squeeze your legs together when you have reached the maximum stretch. The partner resists the push and so keeps your

legs in the position of maximum stretch. When you relax, ask your partner to stretch your legs out a little further.

2. Dynamic stretching

Dynamic stretching describes the ability to move part or parts of the body in a way that requires muscular flexibility. In the static stretch, the position is maintained for a short time. Dynamic stretching only lasts for a moment and is in response to a sudden increase in muscle length. Dynamic stretching is performed once the muscles have warmed up. This form of stretching also increases muscular strength. Dynamic stretching can include exercises such as leg raises and arm swings.

We will now have a look at some stretches that are useful to the Tae Kwon Do student. The method described for each stretch is the static Yoga type of stretch. There is nothing to stop you from experimenting with the other approaches as long as you have a clear understanding of how they work.

i. Stretch for the feet

This stretch is especially useful to help you learn how to curl your toes back for the front kick and turning kick.

1. Kneel on all fours with your toes underneath you. Keep your back straight.

2. Exhale as you force your buttocks backward and downward. You should feel the stretch in the soles of your feet.

ii. Stretch for the calf muscles

This stretch is particularly useful for the calves and Achilles tendon. It can help to reduce the possibility of cramps in the calf muscles.

Bend your body over as shown and support the weight of your body with your arms. Increase the stretch by moving your hands closer to your feet. The foot with the heel down is the one being stretched. You can either stretch both at the same time by having both heels down or one at a time by alternating the feet.

iii. Stretch for hamstrings

This exercise is incorporated into most martial arts stretching routines.

Sit on the floor, with your weight supported by the leg that is flexed. Stabilize the posture by grabbing your ankles. Exhale as you lower your upper torso toward the leg being stretched. You will feel the stretch in the back of your leg.

iv. Stretch for adductors (1)

Strong and supple adductor muscles are essential for side kicks.

Squat with your feet flat on the floor and your toes turned slightly outward. Place your elbows in your thighs. When you exhale, use your elbows to push your thighs out.

v. Stretch for adductors (2)

Sit on the floor and stretch your legs out as far as possible to stretch the inner thigh (adductor). Enhance the stretch by slowly lowering your body to the floor and pushing your hands as far forward as they will go.

vi. Stretch for quadriceps

It is impossible to do a kick without using the quadriceps. This exercise will help keep them supple.

Lie facedown on the floor and grab an ankle. As you exhale, pull your ankle toward your buttock. If your knee feels uncomfortable, stop the exercise. Do not arch your back or twist your lower pelvis.

vii. Stretch for hips and gluteals

Keep your hips supple to avoid hip pain in later life.

Lie on your back with your arms outstretched for stability. Extend your leg. Exhale as you lower the foot toward the opposite hand. Be sure to keep your entire upper trunk and elbows flat on the floor. If your shoulder starts to lift, decrease the range of the stretch by placing your foot in a lower position.

viii. Stretch for lower torso

This stretch is also a part of many Yoga routines and is sometimes called the "Cobra." Lie facedown on the floor. Put your palms next to your waist with your fingers pointing up the length of your body. Simultaneously, exhale and push down with your hands. Arch your back while contracting your buttocks.

ix. Stretch for upper back

It is actually quite difficult to stretch the muscles in the upper back. Try this one.

Interlace your fingers and make your back rounded as shown. Exhale and push your hands forward and back with the muscles in your upper back.

x. Stretch for pectorals

For this exercise, it is best if you have a chair. If one is not available, you can still do the exercise, but it will not be as strong.

Sit on the chair and interlock your hands behind your head. The top of the chair should be around mid-chest level. It is a good idea to place a towel on the top of the chair to stop it from digging into your back. Push your upper torso back and push your elbows backward.

xi. Stretch for shoulders

Some flexible people find this exercise surprisingly difficult. If you are one of them, treat it as any other exercise and work on it gradually.

According to the Yoga guru B.K.S Iyengar, it is the difficult exercises that benefit our bodies the most.

1. Start with your hands behind your back with the palms touching.

2. Inhale as you rotate the wrists so that your fingers are pointing upward.

xii. Stretch for arms and wrists

Be attentive when it comes to arm and wrist stretches. Most of them can double as arm and wrist locks if you apply them to another person. This is one such example.

1. Extend your left arm.

2. Put your right arm under the elbow of your left arm and link your hands.

3. Bring your left hand back so that your right hand can grab your left hand or wrist.

4. Exhale as you press downward lightly with your right hand.

5. Extend as far as you can.

Cardiovascular exercises

If you ever enter a sparring tournament, you will instantly understand why the Tae Kwon Do student must have a high level of cardiovascular fitness. Although the bout may only be three minutes long (two minutes for females), most people finish it with hardly a breath left in their lungs. To be a competent competition fighter, you must work hard on cardiovascular fitness.

What is the best way to work on it? The answer is to train frequently. Cross-training is an excellent way of boosting your fitness. You may not be able to go to the Dojang every night, but there is nothing to stop you from going running, swimming, cycling, or whatever you enjoy. Rowing is excellent for martial artists as it incorporates all of the muscles in the body. The key is in your enjoyment. Be careful when designing a cross-training program and do not forget that the only way to become skilled at Tae Kwon Do is to practice.

The amount of cardiovascular training depends on your aims. If you want to build muscle, keep your cardiovascular training at about 30 minutes, three days a week, to keep your heart in shape without burning too many calories. If you want to lose body fat, start with three days of cardiovascular training and work your way up to four or five days a week for 30 to 45 minutes.

You will need to incorporate cardiovascular training into your routine at home. Your instructor will have a set of exercises that you do in your warm-up session to get the muscles warm. If you are practicing at home, you should really

include some or all of the following exercises to get your heart beating faster.

These exercises have been specifically picked to work with another aspect of your fitness that you will need for Tae Kwon Do training, such as coordination, reflexes, and suppleness. These exercises can be incorporated into a warm-up program.

Cardio exercise 1: jumping jacks

If you need to warm up quickly, a couple of hundred jumping jacks will do the trick. Try to stay light on your feet.

To get the most from the exercise, you should make sure that your hands touch together at the highest point.

1. Start in the attention stance. Jump up and spread your legs as your hands travel upward.

2. Jump back into the attention position.

Cardio exercise 2: running on the spot

Running on the spot is not intended to replace proper running. The idea here is to have a ten-second burst of running as fast as you possibly can. If you want to make the exercise harder, you can always lift the knees higher when you do the running.

A typical running-on-the-spot routine is as follows:

1. 1 minute normal running
2. 30 seconds as fast as you can
3. Normal running for 30 seconds
4. 30 seconds as fast as you can

You can carry on for as long as you want. The trick is to really put the effort into the fast sprints.

Cardio exercise 3: spin jump

This exercise can be used to improve your co-ordination. In Tae Kwon Do, there are many jumping kicks, some of which require jumping and spinning. If you incorporate this exercise into your warm-up routine, your jumping co-ordination will improve.

This is definitely an exercise that you will have to omit if you live in an apartment building—unless you want your neighbors banging their ceilings!

1. Bend your knees. Jump as high as you can and spin through a complete circle.

2. Try to maintain your balance and land as softly as possible.

Cardio exercise 4: tuck jump

This exercise helps you to build up the explosive power in your legs that is vital for powerful kicking.

Bend your knees. Jump as high as you can, but try to tuck yourself into a ball at the top of the jump. It is similar to "bombing" into the swimming pool.

You could try making this harder by combining the spin jump with the tuck jump.

Cardio exercise 5: stretch jump

This exercise is the same as the previous one, except that you expand rather than contract.

Start from a standing position. Jump as high as you can and try to reach upward with your arms as you jump.

Cardio exercise: 6 "cycling"

This exercise is very similar to the idea of running on the spot. All that you need to do is lie on your back and pretend that you are pedaling a bicycle. The part that makes it effective is to use short "sprint" periods, as in the running-on-the-spot exercise.

Cardio exercise 7: shadow boxing

This is often done in Tae Kwon Do classes with the warm-up. All you need to do is keep punching. Try to keep an even rhythm in the beginning. When you have become looser, try sequences of punching quickly and punching slowly, as in the cycling and running on the spot exercises. Try punching in front of a mirror to ensure that you don't drop your guard.

You could also practice some kicking, as shown at the bottom of the page. This has the obvious advantage of improving the speed and power of your punching.

Reverse
hook kick.

Turning kick.

Strength training

If you take a look at most martial artists, you will see a well-developed physique. This does not mean that the Tae Kwon Do student is overly muscular, but the best students appear to be in tip-top condition.

This almost invariably means that the person has been doing some kind of "working out" or strength training. In the old days, there was an opinion that too much gym work would make a person muscle bound and slow. As long as you follow a sensible training routine, you are more likely to strengthen your muscles and improve your overall fitness.

The ideal place to work out is your local gymnasium. Most gym instructors these days are very capable of devising a training program that is suitable for your needs as a Tae Kwon Do student. As muscle mass increases, your metabolic rate will increase, thereby improving your capacity to burn more calories.

It may be that you do not actually live near a gym or cannot attend for some other reason, such as time or financial constraints. This need not be a barrier to your training.

If you want to buy some equipment to use at home, an ideal tool is the "gym ball." The gym ball was originally used for people who were in rehabilitation for various injuries. It is basically like a large beach ball that you can use as part of your exercise routine. And, more importantly, it is cheap!

The advantage of the gym ball is that it forces you to use your stabilizing or core muscles. As their name suggests, these muscles are deeper inside your body than the exterior sets. If you can improve the quality of your core muscles, you will help your balance and strength.

One myth associated with strength training is that muscle size will increase excessively. Muscle size is primarily affected by genetics and hormone production. Bodybuilders spend hours in the gym every day; they don't acquire their physique accidentally. They follow very specialized and strict training regimes.

The following exercises provide useful techniques for building up your strength at home. An important part of strength training is to keep the exercise routine varied, as your body responds well to that. Try different combinations of the exercises. Be creative!

Strength exercise 1: the push-up

The push-up is an old favorite in most fitness routines. It is a good, simple exercise that works very well. It is also a good indicator of your upper-body strength. Good upper-body strength and arm movement can help you move the whole of your body more fluidly.

There are many different versions of the push-up such as one-armed, on hands, on knuckles, etc. We will look at basic push-ups, as well as a few other suggestions.

1. Lie on the floor with your hands on the floor beside your shoulders. Straighten your arms to push your body up. Keep your back straight.

2. Lower your body by bending your elbows until your chest is close to the floor. This is a complete push-up.

Other suggestions

If you find the push-up difficult, try push-ups from the knees.

If you find the push-up easy, try raising your feet (put them on a solid box or a step). The higher their position, the more difficult the push-up.

If you want to toughen your knuckles for board breaking, try push-ups on your fists.

Remember that the pressure should be on the two front knuckles that you punch with (see page 123).

Bring your hands close together to focus the exercise into your tricep muscles.

Position your hands wide apart to focus the exercise into your chest muscles.

Variants with a gym ball:

Try doing the push-up with your hands on the gym ball. You will find this is more difficult than it looks.

If you have well-developed upper-body strength, try putting your feet on the gym ball.

Strength exercise 2: the crunch

Strong abdominal muscles are the center of your movement in martial arts. If your abdominal muscles are weak, then it is more difficult for your back to support your weight. The result can be bad posture.

If your posture is bad, then your center of gravity will rise, and it will be more difficult to balance your body. Poor balance means that it is hard to generate power in punches and kicks.

In the crunch, your muscles are flexed, but you do not have to lift your whole body up. This is the most efficient way of doing your sit-ups.

Notice that the head is free. Old-school sit-ups encouraged the support of the back of the head. This can cause injury to your neck if you pull too hard.

1. Lie on the floor with your back flat and your knees up. Your arms are at your sides.

2. Lift your shoulders from the floor and slide your hands forward. Your hands should slide approximately 3–4 inches (8–10 cm). This is one crunch.

Variations

There are other variations on the sit-up that you may wish to try.

Work the oblique muscles by pushing your left shoulder toward your right knee and vice versa.

Work higher in the abdomen by raising the knees and buttocks for the exercise.

Gym ball variation

Lean back on the gym ball and do the crunch in the same way. Note that the hands are near the head but not actually making contact. Do not overextend your back by leaning backward too far.

Strength exercise 3: the plank

This exercise is so called because your body should be straight like a plank when you do it. It is excellent for working your abdominal and back muscles.

1. Lie on the floor on your belly. Touch your hands under your body in a "praying" position. Touch the floor with the balls of your feet.

2. Lift your body with your abdominal muscles and hold it there. Keep your back straight. Keep your breath steady and even.

Variation

Try exercising the muscles on the sides of your body in the same way (shown below). If you attempt this exercise, be sure that you can keep your back straight while doing it.

Gym ball variation

This is an excellent exercise for the gym ball. You do exactly the same exercise, but rest your elbows and forearms on the gym ball. It is easier if you link your hands together because the structure is more stable. When you are accustomed to the exercise, you will no longer need to link your hands.

The variation from the side can also be done on the Swiss ball—this will really test your balance!

Strength exercise 4: reverse plank

The reverse plank exercise works in much the same way as the plank exercise, except that it is the other way around. This position reversal means that the back muscles are emphasized more than the abdominal muscles although both are used.

1. Lie on your back with your arms at your sides and your knees bent. Tuck your feet in so that they are fairly close to your buttocks.

2. Use your legs and abdominal muscles to lift your body. Keep your back straight by clenching the buttocks.

Variation

If you like this exercise, you can extend it into the Yogic exercise called "the bridge" by placing your hands behind your shoulders and lifting the upper part of your body

Gym ball variation

To do this exercise with a gym ball, you are effectively doing the "bridge" exercise with the ball to support your upper middle back. Once the exercise has become easy, you can increase the pressure by placing a heavy book or small weight on your abdominal area.

Strength exercise 5: grip

When you make a fist, it is not just the muscles in your hands that are involved. If you clench your fist tightly, you will be able to feel the muscles in your forearms contracting.

1. Hold your hands out in front of your body.

The stronger the muscles in the hands and forearms, the tighter you will be able to contract the fist for the moment of impact. In Tae Kwon Do, your fist is tightly clenched to make the impact stronger.

The following exercise is good for working these muscles. It has an added benefit. In traditional Chinese and Japanese medicine, there is a whole collection of energy channels or meridians that finish in the fingers. This exercise helps you to "pump" the meridians and enhance the flow of energy in a positive way.

Increase the repetitions as your muscles become accustomed to the exercise. Do not worry if it makes your hands feel like jelly in the beginning!

Variation

There are just as many energy meridians and muscles in the feet as the hands. Try sitting with your legs outstretched and do the same exercise with your toes. This is another exercise that you could probably get away with while sitting at your desk!

2. Clench the fist and release. Repeat ten times.

3. Repeat holding the hands to the sides.

5. Repeat holding the hands behind your body.

4. Repeat holding the hands high.

Meditation

I have discussed with many martial artists from Korea, Japan, and China what they think the main differences are between training in the West and training in the East. One of the most common things they mention is meditation.

In the West, we commonly do not make time for meditation and, therefore, lose out on the benefits. Among the many benefits of meditation are a reduction in stress (therefore strengthening the immune system) and clarity of thought.

Clarity of thought is a really useful concept in Tae Kwon Do. If you imagine that you are trying to break something with your punch, you must focus your mind. The same applies to poomsae and sparring. If you cannot focus your mind, you will sooner or later reach a point beyond which you cannot progress.

Meditation is like weight lifting for the mind. In the beginning, it may feel odd to sit there, trying to empty your mind and think nothing. It may even feel pointless until you have felt the really refreshing results.

If you can only manage to meditate for a few minutes, then so be it! You can work on it the same way that you would anything else—gradually. If you find meditation difficult in the beginning, it is probably what your mind and body need. Great fruits will be reaped!

There are many methods of meditation. Practicing Tae Kwon Do is actually one of them. We will take a look at a very simple but effective meditation method called "breathing into the Danjon."

Meditation reduces stress, encourages relaxation, and improves clarity of thought.

Breathing into the Danjon

As mentioned previously, the Danjon is the body's "energetic" center. Focusing your breathing into that area is useful for calming your energy. You may find this technique especially useful if your daily routine forces you to train at night. It will help you to calm your body and mind and aid restful sleep.

1. Sit down in the kneeling position shown, with your hands gently resting on your abdomen, just below your navel. If this makes your knees uncomfortable, try sitting on cushions or cross-legged. The kneeling position is popular because it gives you a firm base to support your back and keep it straight. As long as your back is straight, you will be comfortable and well balanced.

2. Close your eyes and listen to your breathing. Is it fast, slow, regular, irregular, deep, or shallow? Do not judge, just notice.

3. Now bring your attention down to the point where your hands are resting on your abdomen. When you breathe in and out, do your hands move?

4. Gently try to adjust your breathing rhythm so that your hands move outward when you inhale and inward when you exhale. You are now doing abdominal breathing—a popular technique in martial arts and Yoga.

5. Carry on with the abdominal breathing for a few deep breaths. Feel the air going deep into your lungs. Imagine that you are breathing down into your abdomen.

6. After a few good, deep breaths to clear the lungs, breathe more gently. Try to make the breathing as smooth and deep as you can. This should be a very gentle stage of the meditation. Imagine that the point under your hands is becoming denser as you breathe into it.

7. Try to make your breathing silent but deep. Continue with the visualization that you are bringing energy into your Danjon.

8. When you have had enough, gently bring yourself out of the meditation. Shake your body about to bring it back to life again and distribute the Ki.

Chapter 5

Stepping and stances

One of the most important aspects of martial arts training, whether it is Tae Kwon Do or any other style, is the footwork. If your footwork is not good, then you need to work on it. No successful martial artist ever considered footwork to be unimportant.

Imagine a cannon on a ship or castle. When a cannonball is fired, the force from the explosion causes the cannon to move backward if it is not held down. This is one of the principles upon which Tae Kwon Do stances are based. If you fire out your fist like a cannonball and your feet slide backward from the force, you have lost some of the impact energy.

If the punch makes contact, then the backward reaction will be greater. If the reaction force knocks you off balance or throws you back, you will be in a more vulnerable position than before you threw the punch.

The solution is to use a good, strong stance that can withstand the impact of the reaction to your techniques. The stances in Tae Kwon Do are similar to those in many martial arts.

Once you have learned how to use steady stances, think about how to move in that stance. If you are rooted to the spot, you will not be much of a martial artist. When stepping and in transition between the stances, you should try to be well balanced.

Stepping and stance training is the key to distancing yourself from the attacker. If you are good with your footwork, it is possible to put a person off balance just by stepping to him or her in the correct way. Clearly, correct footwork is an aspect of the art that will be refined throughout your progression. The way that you understand your footwork in a year's time should be different from your comprehension at the present moment.

Ready stance: jumbi seogi

The jumbi stance is used at the beginning of a class after the bow is made to the instructor. It is also used at the beginning of all Taegeuk poomsae and other formal exercises.

Your body should be straight and in good alignment. This shows that you have strong spirit. Stay alert when in the stance. If you allow your mind to drift when in the stance before performing poomsae at a grading, for example, your instructor will notice. You will have made your first mistake before actually doing anything. Tae Kwon Do is as much about state of mind as body!

Jumbi seogi is a neutral stance that is neither aggressive nor retreating. Your feet should be shoulder width apart, held parallel and pointing forward. Your body weight should be evenly distributed on both feet.

We will look at how to get into jumbi from the attention stance.

1. Stand to attention with your arms at the sides of your body and feet together.

2. Raise the forearms in front of your body with your hands held as a fist, palm facing upward. As you are raising your fists, step with the left foot to shoulder width and lower the arms to the correct position.

Horse-riding stance: joochoom seogi

In this stance, you should look like somebody riding a horse, and this is not just from the position of the legs. Good riders make an effort to keep their backs straight, and it is essential in this stance.

The inner edges of your feet are parallel and approximately 2 feet apart. You need to bend your knees slightly and direct your body weight inward. Your weight should be distributed equally between your feet. Keep the shin in a vertical position.

This stance is really stable and is very useful for both attacks and defense. It can be very difficult for beginners because it is demanding on the muscles. Try standing in the posture for a few minutes a day to build up your strength.

Walking stance: ap seogi

The walking stance is probably the most natural in the martial arts spectrum. It is exactly what it says—the stance that we use for walking.

In the walking stance, your weight is higher than it is in the front stance, so it is more difficult to generate as much power. However, it has the advantage of being more natural for the body. If you were in a potentially aggressive situation, then you could adopt a good walking stance without anybody noticing. This gives you the extra benefit that you can fall back on to your training without being aggressive or obvious.

If you were to try to go into a long stance in normal life, you would not look natural and could antagonize a potential threat into becoming an actual threat.

In the walking stance, your feet should be shoulder width apart and pointing straight forward. Your weight should be evenly distributed between both feet.

Front stance: apkubi seogi

The front stance is a strong attacking stance that can also be used when blocking. The strength of the stance is in pushing your energy and strength forward, hence its obvious application for attacking. It can also be used to make a retreat. If you are in a situation where you need to retreat but also want to give a show of strength, you can step backward in the front stance.

Your weight should be evenly distributed on both feet. The stance is around shoulder width wide and one-and-a-half shoulder widths in length. Your front leg should be bent at the knee and your back leg straight. Your hips should face forward. Both feet should stay flat on the floor. Keep both of your feet facing forward and parallel to each other.

Stepping in front stance

To continue stepping, follow the sequence.

If you want to step backward in the back stance, it is exactly the same. Just follow the instructions in reverse. The same pictures will apply.

When stepping, ensure that you move your feet forward in a straight line. You can do this by imagining that your feet are moving along parallel railway lines.

Your head should remain at the same height. You achieve this by bending at the knees, rather than straightening the legs as you move forward.

1. Start in ready stance (jumbi seogi).

2. Move your left leg forward and bend your leg at the knee into front stance.

3. Keep your left leg bent as you bring your right foot forward. The foot travels forward in a straight line. Keep the knees bent so that the head remains at a constant height. Be careful to keep your balance, so that you do not wobble.

4. Step forward with the right foot into the next front stance in a straight line. To continue stepping, repeat the sequence.

Back stance: dwit kubi seogi

The back stance is primarily a defensive stance.

In this stance, two-thirds of the weight is placed on the back leg. The heels should be in line with each other. The front foot is straight, but this time the back foot is at a 90-degree angle to the front foot. The front foot should be one step away from the back foot. The body is lowered slightly by bending both of the knees.

This stance places stress on the standing leg because it compresses all of the muscles in that leg. As you start to tire, be careful that you do not lean forward and put too much weight on your front leg or allow the knee to collapse. Remember your Tae Kwon Do spirit! After training, your muscles will become accustomed to the stance, and it will not feel difficult.

The fact that most of your weight is on the rear leg means that you can quickly pick up the leading leg for a front kick. This is a useful trick that can change your retreat into an attack. It also puts you in a good position to power forward from your rear leg into an attacking front stance.

Stepping in the back stance

1. Start in the ready stance.

2. Open the right foot to a 90-degree angle as you bend both knees.

3. Move your left foot forward in line with your right heel.

As with the front stance, remember to keep your head at the same height and don't allow it to move up and down as you are stepping forward.

4. Move your right foot close to your left foot. Turn your left foot through a 90-degree angle.

5. Step forward with your right foot.

Tiger stance: beom seogi

The tiger stance is so called because it is said to resemble the way a tiger steps. A tiger will test the ground with its foot before putting weight on it. In the tiger stance, all of your weight is on the rear standing leg, while the ball of the leading foot gently touches the floor.

The main usage for this stance is for when you need to suddenly move your body backward in a defensive posture. If you step back in the tiger stance, your front leg is in an ideal position to deliver a front kick.

It is not usually a stance that is used for stepping in kyorugi (sparring), although some clubs may step in the tiger stance just to train the legs.

Place the leading foot one foot's distance forward. Move the back foot so that it is at an angle of 45 degrees to the front foot. The back leg supports the entire weight of the body. The knees are kept bent, thereby lowering the body. The front foot is stretched so that only the ball of the foot rests on the floor.

Chapter 6 **Basic techniques**

Basic techniques are the foundation of the martial art of Tae Kwon Do. The only way to learn them is through repetition until the technique becomes a natural movement.

Tae Kwon Do techniques are used either to strike an opponent or to evade a strike. When your understanding becomes deeper, you will learn that blocks can be used as strikes and vice versa. Some of the basic techniques can also be used as locks or throws. For now, we will look at a single application for each technique. Always try to think of new applications for the techniques, as this will improve your Tae Kwon Do and help you learn more effectively.

Repetition and practice will make your basic techniques strong and accurate. Basic techniques are the building blocks of Tae Kwon Do. It is of little use if you know lots of different poomsae (routines) but are unable to punch your way out of a paper bag. A good technique can be used for poomsae, sparring, and self-defense training.

The art of breath control

Breath control is the ability to synchronize your breathing with your technique. On a basic level, this means that you exhale for outward movements and inhale when the movement is coming back to you.

Consider the punch, for example. Without trying to control it, just let a few punches out now taking note of your breathing. Most people will find that when you punch, you exhale. This makes it obvious that for the time in between the punches where you pull your fists back ready to strike again, you inhale.

If you can coordinate your breathing with your movements, you will have a connection between the external part of the movement—i.e., the punch—and the internal part, namely the breathing.

Now we have our first difficulty. That is, trying too hard. The breathing should be entirely natural in the beginning and not forced. People who worry too much about breathing in the early days normally find themselves in all sorts of confusion. It is quite common to see Tae Kwon Do students perform the whole of Taeguk 1 without breathing!

But there is more to breath control than just this. When you have been practicing for a while, and your mind has learned to let your body take over, there is a next level.

A famous legend in martial arts is the "one inch punch" performed by Bruce Lee. Many think that just because Bruce Lee did the punch that it belongs exclusively to the Chinese styles.

The first thing to ask is how did he do it? Now imagine that you could perform breath control at an advanced level. This would mean that you would be able to focus all of your breath and power into a short distance. The advanced Tae Kwon Do student does this at the end of every punch. Observers will sometimes see this as a "snap" at the end of a technique.

What happens is that very close to the end of the punch, all of the muscles become momentarily tense and the breath is forced out in a short burst. Another effect is that the mind becomes wonderfully focused on the technique that you are doing. So, in short, the breath control is the combination of body movement, breath control, and intent of the mind all in one short burst.

You should try to do the breath control at the end of every block, strike, punch, or kick in your Tae Kwon Do. It is common that this short burst of breath can make the person produce an audible noise as the air blasts through the lungs. This brings us to the next point—"kihap."

Kihap

If you stand outside a Tae Kwon Do class, you will usually hear a lot of shouting (unless the walls are soundproof). This is not just because they are having fun—although let's hope that they are! The Tae Kwon Do students are using a technique called "kihap." Many martial arts use the technique, although some call it by a different name.

Why do it? It is partly an extension of breath control. If you shout with a technique, then it forces all of the air out of your lungs and constricts the abdomen. Both are essential ingredients for breath control.

But there is another reason for using breath control. If you are on the attack and simultaneously yell, then it can frighten the opponent. As you are in a fighting situation, you need all of the advantages that you can get.

It also gives the attacker a psychological advantage, and the surprise it generates may provide a vital moment when you can prepare your next move. If all it takes to gain half a second is a good loud shout, then it is worth trying. In half a second, you can deliver a knockout blow!

A loud kihap demonstrates a strong fighting spirit.

Striking areas

If you go into a martial arts store, the chances are that you will see some kind of poster that illustrates the "vital points" that you need for Tae Kwon Do. These points are usually at acupuncture points called "kup-so." Frequently, a point will also be on a place that common sense tells you to protect, such as the ear or the eye.

The idea of these vital points is that they are targets for you to aim your strikes at. Frequently, there will also be a description of the best way to hit that point.

These charts are generally for the highly advanced student. For example, there are hundreds of points around the head and neck. If you get a good strike to the area with something like a reverse knife-hand strike, it matters very little which one you have hit.

There is also an idea that if your technique is good and your intention powerful, it matters very little where you hit the opponent, but how you hit them is critical. Again, this is a more advanced concept in Tae Kwon Do.

For those who wish to know more about the points and how to use them, a Shiatsu book is a good place to start.

Many techniques can be used to strike the vital areas, for example the punch (see right) can be used to attack the solar plexus. Similarly, the solar plexus can be attacked using a spear finger strike (see page 150) or a kicking technique. The technique that you use to strike the vital areas depends on many factors, such as the attacker's position or stance, his or her

Making contact with the large knuckles of the fist maximizes the striking power of the punch.

attack (whether it is a kick or a punch), distance from the attacker, the techniques that you prefer to use, and the vital areas that the attacker has left vulnerable to your strike. One of the most important skills that a martial artist will develop is the ability to quickly assess easy target areas of the opponent.

The punch making contact with a vital point—the solar plexus.

Attacking techniques (kongkyok kisul)

Punching (jireugi)

Everybody knows how to punch! Well, that is what a lot of people think at first. You just clench your fist and let rip! But along with that instinctive knowledge, we also know that some people are better at punching than others.

In Tae Kwon Do, the mechanics of the punch are examined in fine detail. We find that what starts off as a basic movement that everybody understands can be refined to a high level. Which part of the hand do you punch with? Where do you punch? Where does the power come from? What range does the punch have?

These are all questions that the Tae Kwon Do student must be able to answer about his or her punches. But remember, no amount of understanding and analysis with the mind can replace practice! It is also worth noting that, in the World Tae Kwon Do Federation style of full-contact sparring, punching to the head is an illegal attack.

	Points to remember about punching
1	Punches travel in a straight line from the waist to the target.
2	There should always be a reaction hand for the punch—that is, you pull one hand back as you punch with the other.
3	Sink your hips every time you strike.
4	Exhale on the punch.
5	The fist twists at the end of the punch to increase power.
6	The elbow is bent at the beginning of the punch but straightens at the end. This adds power to the punch.
7	Timing is crucial.
8	The power of the punch can be increased by moving the body forward.

Making a fist (jumeok)

Making a fist is probably one of the most basic of human reactions. If you are on a roller coaster ride, when the cars suddenly shoot down one of the slopes, the chances are that you will have made a fist. It's also likely that the fist is formed correctly.

Sometimes when you overanalyze things, they can get mixed up. If you are working from a pure "gut reaction," as you are when the roller coaster is tumbling down the hill, your mind has not confused things by analyzing exactly which is the best way to place your fingers.

Some strikes will use specialized fists with a protruding knuckle, but these fists are not within the scope of this basic Tae Kwon Do book.

1. Open your hand.

2. Bend the fingers.

3. Tuck the fingers tightly into the palm.

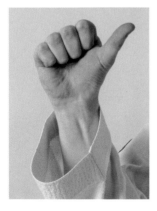

4. Fold the thumb over tightly— remember to keep your thumb tight, as it is easy to catch and break the thumb when sparring if it is not kept out of the way.

The strike area is the two largest knuckles. There should be a straight line between the two largest knuckles and your forearm.

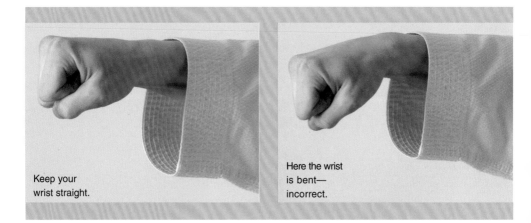

Keep your wrist straight.

Here the wrist is bent— incorrect.

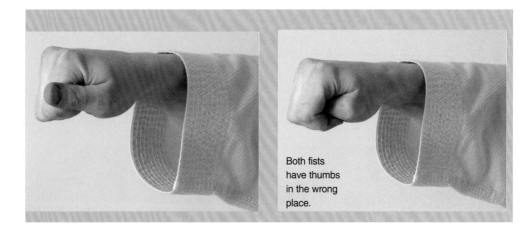

Both fists have thumbs in the wrong place.

The straight punch: bandae jireugi

1	contact area	two front knuckles
2	range	medium to long
3	target area	anywhere!
4	power	strong
5	speed	medium to fast
6	difficulty level	easy
7	suitability for sparring	n/a

This punch is the basic building block of many of the other punches. It is fairly fast and has the power to stop an opponent. It is versatile and can be used on any target.

The most difficult part of this punch are timing the left hand with the right hand (both should move at the same speed) and getting the twist at the end of the punch.

The punch is shown here in the ready stance. If it were done in the front stance, it would become another punch. It could also be done in the back stance.

Punches can be classified according to the height of the punch.

1. Face punch (olgul jireugi): the target area is the head.

2. Body punch (momtong jireugi): the target is the solar plexus.

3. Low punch (arae jireugi): the target area is the "danjon" (the lower part of abdomen).

Stepping punch

1	contact area	two largest knuckles
2	range	long
3	target area	frequently mid-section but can be used anywhere
4	power	very strong; it has the weight of your body behind it
5	speed	medium
6	difficulty level	easy, but requires coordination of the arms and legs
7	suitability for sparring	good

If you step forward in the front stance while executing a straight punch, you will have done a stepping punch. This is used to get nearer to the opponent to hit him or her.

It is very powerful because it should have the whole of your body weight concentrated into a small striking area. It is not as fast as the jireugi (straight) punch because you need to step to perform it. As with all punches, timing is the key to power!

1. Start in the ready stance.

2. Raise your right arm as you step up with your left fist.

3. Step forward with your left leg into the front stance. Twist your body and pull back with your right arm as you punch with your left fist.

Cross punch

1	contact area	two largest knuckles
2	range	short/medium
3	target area	head/chin
4	power	strong
5	speed	fast
6	difficulty level	easy, but requires practice to generate a powerful punch
7	suitability for sparring	not used in full-contact Tae Kwon Do sparring

The cross punch is very similar to the jab. The difference is that you punch with the reverse (in this case the right hand), rather than the leading hand (same side as the forward foot). This allows you to twist your body into the punch to generate power, but it is slightly slower than the jab. When punching, always bring your punching hand straight back to its guard position.

1. Start in fighting stance with the right leg back and the guard held up.

2. Punch with the right hand. While punching, ensure that the hips twist and that the right foot rotates to generate power into the punch.

Reverse punch: baro jireugi

1	contact area	two front knuckles
2	range	medium to long
3	target area	middle section or high section
4	power	very strong; it is usually the strongest punch
5	speed	medium to fast
6	difficulty level	easy, but power must come from the waist
7	suitability for sparring	n/a

If you have ever been to a Tae Kwon Do display where the student and the instructor are demonstrating their power by breaking slabs of wood with a punch, it is highly likely that this was the punch used.

It is relatively simple to learn and VERY powerful. The key to this punch is the same as all of the others: coordination of the punch with the movement of the waist, backed up by the use of the reaction arm.

Remember that extra power is available if you time your exhalation to coincide with the outward movement of the punch.

The reverse punch lends itself ideally as a follow-up technique in combination with the jabbing punch.

Here the heel is lifting—this will weaken the move.

Start in the left front stance with your left arm extended. Pull your left elbow back as you start to punch with the right fist. Continue the pull with your left elbow as you push the punch forward. The punch finishes as you twist your hips into the final position. The movement of both fists should finish simultaneously with the twist. Your right fist twists as you exhale on the last moment.

The reverse punch is so called because the opposite arm and leg are forward. If your left leg is forward, your right fist should be extended, and vice versa. The same logic applies to other techniques, such as the reverse knife-hand.

If your punching arm is the same as the forward leg, you are performing a forward punch.

Jabbing punch

1	contact area	ideally two front knuckles, but whole of the front fist is common in sparring
2	range	short to medium
3	target area	head
4	power	least powerful, but can still have quite a sting!
5	speed	medium to fast
6	difficulty level	easy, but power must come from the waist
7	suitability for sparring	good, but be careful where the tournament rules dictate that you cannot punch to the head

Every boxer needs to develop a good jab. This is not because you will normally score a knockout blow with a jab, although this has happened. It is because a good, fast, powerful jab opens the way for a more powerful technique, like a kick.

Some tournament fighters like the jab-jab-punch rhythm. In this, the two leading jabs are used to open the defenses, and the final punch is where he or she gets the score, so watch out for it! Remember that punches to the head are not permitted in the rule of the World Tae Kwon Do Federation (WTF).

The essence of the jab is the same as that performed by a boxer. Watch and learn from boxers on TV, as they are normally the best at it!

The jab is a very simple punch that is done by an extension of the arm. Do not forget your waist rotation, as, without it, there is hardly any power. Note that the reaction hand is hardly used for the jabbing punch. Always remember your guard when punching.

The jabbing punch is a fast technique, so stay light on your feet.

A variation of the jab punch is the stepping jab punch. The mechanics are the same, but you step forward into the front stance as you throw the punch.

1. Start in a fight stance.

2. Extend the hand in front of you in a snapping motion. Keep the elbow pointing downward and use the two largest knuckles to make contact.

Hooking punch: dollyo jireugi

1	contact area	ideally, two front knuckles, but whole of the front fist is common in sparring
2	range	short
3	target area	head, sometimes used for middle section
4	power	medium
5	speed	slow to medium
6	difficulty level	easy; requires coordination with the reaction hand
7	suitability for sparring	good for semi-contact, limited for full contact

This is another punching technique that boxers use in their sport. It is also commonly used by people untrained in martial arts. If you are unfortunate enough to have seen a fight in real life, the chances are that there would be very little real technique involved, but the one punch you may see is the hooking punch.

It is less common in martial arts, because it is relatively easy to block. One of the reasons for this is that it travels in a semicircle. Most Tae Kwon Do punches travel in a straight line—the shortest way to get between two points. This can mean that the fighter who is limited only to hooking punches will be slower than those able to execute straight punches. Moreover, the straight punch will get straight through to the target.

This all makes the hooking punch look very unattractive, but that is because many do not understand its tactical use. If you are very close to your opponent, it can sometimes be a very useful option. And then it is both difficult to anticipate and hard to block—a winning combination.

The hooking punch is a close fighting technique. If you find that you have to lean into it to hit the target, you need to either get closer to the target or use another punch with a greater range.

Try practicing the hook punch with combinations of jabbing punches and straight punches.

1. Start in the fighting stance.

2. Turn your waist to the right and allow your left arm to extend; pull your right elbow back. Twist your waist back to the left as you pull your left elbow back and punch with your right fist. Exhale on the punch.

Uppercut punch: chi jireugi

1	**contact area**	two front knuckles
2	**range**	short
3	**target area**	chin or solar plexus
4	**power**	medium
5	**speed**	fast
6	**difficulty level**	easy
7	**suitability for sparring**	reasonable—in WTF tournaments it is unlikely to score a point, but can be useful to keep an opponent back.

If you imagine performing a hooking punch on a vertical rather than a horizontal plane, you will be close to the uppercut punch.

The classic target for the uppercut punch is the point of the chin, as used in boxing. This technique is useful for self-defense but is impractical for tournament sparring.

To get maximum power into the punch, you must coordinate both arms and shift your body weight with the punch to drive it through. This is how boxers inflict damaging body blows or score a knockout with the punch.

The punch can be done from either the leading or trailing fist.

1. Start in the fighting stance.

2. Drive the punching fist forward as you pull the other one back.

Striking: chigi

Tae Kwon Do has a wide variety of striking techniques, as well as punching techniques.

The aim in striking is to use one of your contact areas for attacking against a strike area on the opponent. Many of the striking techniques come from the realm of unarmed combat rather than competition. For example, a high-powered knife-hand strike to the neck can easily result in permanent injury or even death!

The techniques are a valuable part of Tae Kwon Do, however, and vital ingredients to the Tae Kwon Do "spirit." In your classes, they will be studied either in poomsae or one-step sparring.

We shall examine both closed- and open-handed strikes. The striking areas for the open-hand can be either the edge of the hand, the finger tips, or the heel of the palm.

Striking techniques used in Tae Kwon Do are very powerful and are an important part of training.

The back fist

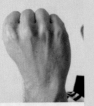

1	contact area	back of the two front knuckles
2	range	short to medium
3	target area	temples or jaw
4	power	medium
5	speed	fast
6	difficulty level	easy
7	suitability for sparring	not good, as it can be a dangerous technique

The back fist does not have the same amount of power as the reverse punch or front punch. However, it still has enough power to be used as a destructive technique.

It is used for short- to middle-range attacks and can be used to unfold an attack from inside the opponent's guard.

Outer back fist strike (olgul bakkat chigi)

This technique is used to attack the temple or jaw.

1. Start in the ready stance. The motion of this strike is similar to the outer block (see page 182).

2. Move the palm of the left fist across your body with the right arm extended.

3. Pull your right elbow back as you strike toward the temple with the back of your left fist.

The back fist can be used to strike the temple or jaw (olgul bakkat chigi) or the front of the face (apchigi). The only thing that really changes is the plane of attack. To attack the face, the fist moves vertically. To attack the temple, the fist moves close to horizontally.

Face back fist (apchigi)

This technique is used to attack the front of the face.

1. Start in the ready stance.

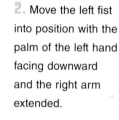

2. Move the left fist into position with the palm of the left hand facing downward and the right arm extended.

3. The striking hand goes straight forward toward the target.

Hammer fist strike: mejumeok chigi

1	contact area	bottom of fist
2	range	short to medium
3	target area	any part of the body
4	power	high
5	speed	medium–fast
6	difficulty level	easy
7	suitability for sparring	can be used with control, but check the rule book

The hammer fist strike could be used to give a jarring blow to the head or to attack a collarbone. Other strike areas will work, but these are the ones to watch out for in poomsae and one-step sparring.

It is a circular technique. This means that the momentum is not built in a straight line like many of the techniques, but by making a circle with your fist. It can be very powerful.

As it is a circular movement, it can be used to great effect when attacking from inside an opponent's guard. Upon completion of the technique, your elbow should be straight.

The hammer fist strike can be used on the vertical, horizontal, or inclined planes.

If the angle of attack is changed, it can be used to attack the sides of the body—just imagine that you are using your fist like a hammer!

1. Start in the front stance in the low block position.

2. Pull back as you rotate your forearm. Pull your fist around in a circle.

3. Pull the fist downward to strike.

Knife-hand strike: sonnal mok chigi

1	contact area	edge of hand, on the side of the little finger
2	range	medium to long
3	target area	sides of the body, usually neck or temple
4	power	high
5	speed	medium–fast
6	difficulty level	medium
7	suitability for sparring	not suitable for free sparring

Some techniques in Tae Kwon Do are just too dangerous for free sparring. The knife-hand strikes usually fall into this category. In sparring, it is possible to make mistakes—as in anything else. A bad mistake with a knife-hand technique can result in a serious injury. It is also worth bearing this fact in mind if you ever need to use the technique to defend yourself.

The technique uses the edge of the hand as shown and lends itself to attacking the sides of the body. The momentum comes from a circular motion that starts either behind your head or in font of the body.

The technique can be done either as a stepping technique or as a standing technique in any of the stances.

Outside knife-hand (sonnal mok chigi)
Strike from the ready stance

1. Ready stance.

2. Extend your left hand and raise your right hand behind your head. Pull your left hand back as your right hand starts to move. Continue the path with both hands; make a fist with the left hand.

3. Snap the technique into the finish position as your left fist finishes in front stance. Your right palm faces upward.

Inside knife-hand strike: sonnal bakkat chigi

The outside knife-hand strike previously described is called an outside technique because it starts on the outside of your body (logical really!). There is nothing stopping you from using the same strike from the inside of your body. In this case, it is called the inside knife-hand strike.

The technique uses the same part of the hand for striking, except that the hand is the other way up at the finish. The applications are the same.

1. Ready stance.

2. Start with your left arm extended with the palm of your right hand facing your face. Pull your left elbow back as your right arm starts to move outward.

3. Continue the path with both hands. Make a fist with your left hand.

4. Extend and snap into the technique with your right hand as your left fist finishes.

Reverse knife-hand strike (or ridge hand): sonnal deung chigi

1	contact area	edge of hand, on the side of the thumb
2	range	medium to long
3	target area	sides of the body, usually neck or temple
4	power	high
5	speed	medium fast
6	difficulty level	easy
7	suitability for sparring	not suitable for free sparring

This knife-hand technique uses the opposite side of the hand to the previous knife-hand technique. Be sure that when you use the technique that you get your thumb well out of the way. If you do not, it can cause painful injuries even if you are only hitting a punching bag.

If facing on to your opponent, the attack areas will be the neck and the temple. If you are sideways to your opponent, then the bridge of the nose is a good target area.

This is a very powerful technique that is frequently used for breaking wood.

Ridge hand strike from the ready stance

1. Ready stance.

2 Extend your right hand in front of yourself and your left hand to the side.

3. Pull back with your left hand as your right hand starts to travel. Make a fist with your left hand.

4. As you extend and snap your right hand into the technique, twist your left fist. Remember that power comes from the waist! Twist into front stance.

Elbowing techniques: palkup

1	contact area	edge of elbow or point of elbow
2	range	close to medium
3	target area	jaw or chin
4	power	very high
5	speed	medium–fast
6	difficulty level	easy
7	suitability for sparring	not suitable for free sparring

Most of the punching and striking techniques shown so far have been for medium- or long-range attacks. If your opponent comes inside that circle of attack, however, many of the attacks will be difficult for you to execute.

However, this does not mean that you are beaten! Your Tae Kwon Do spirit should be stronger than that. On the inner circle, you will use your elbows and knees.

Elbow and knee attacks can be very powerful. In Tae Kwon Do, they are not usually used for free sparring. Thai boxers will use elbows and knees, but these fighters have usually undergone intense physical and mental conditioning to withstand the blow. Even then, it is not uncommon for injuries to happen in that environment.

There are several possible attacks with the elbow. We will have a look at some of the more common ones. They are usually semicircular or stabbing techniques. The main difference between them is the direction in which they travel. They are all devastating!

Upper elbow strike (palkup ollyo chigi)

The upper elbow strike follows very similar dynamics to an uppercut punch. If it helps in the beginning, you can imagine this technique as punching with the elbow.

It uses the edge of the elbow to connect with the point of the opponent's chin.

If you can catapult the strike from your hips, you will add more power to the technique.

1. Ready stance.

2. Extend your left fist. Pull back the left fist as the right fist starts to travel forward. Start to lift the right elbow.

3. Power the right elbow into a high finishing position as the left fist snaps to the waist. Finish in front stance.

Elbow strike (palkup dollyo chigi)

This powerful technique could be aimed high to the side of the head or lower to the sides of the body and the floating rib. This is the most common version of the elbow attack.

It follows very similar mechanics to the hooking punch.

The technique can be made even more devastating by placing the non-striking hand around the back of your attacker's head (known as palkup pyojeok chigi). This means that the full impact of the strike is absorbed by the target area.

1. Ready stance.

2. Extend your right hand. As you start to pull your right fist back, your left fist starts to make an arc. Continue the arc as though punching to your throat with a hooking punch.

3. Extend the left elbow as you pull your right hand back.

Reverse middle elbow strike: palkup dwiro chigi

This strike uses the point of the elbow to attack an opponent who is behind you. It will hit the attacker in either the solar plexus or the ribs.

It is a common self-defense technique against attackers who grab you from behind.

On the arm that uses the elbow for the attack, the fist is clenched. The other palm is placed on the top of the fist to give it extra strength and drive the attack home.

1. Ready stance.

2. Extend your left fist. Place your right hand over your left fist.

3. Push the left elbow back. Drive the attack home with a movement of the waist. Finish in horse-riding stance.

Other strikes

The strikes shown here are by no means exhaustive—there is a vast range of strikes available to the advanced Tae Kwon Do student. They do, however, show the mechanics of some of them.

Once you have grasped the mechanics of the movement, it is possible to learn new strikes just by knowing the part of the body you are striking with, where you are striking to, and an idea of how it is done.

We will look briefly at some of the other strikes that are used in Tae Kwon Do.

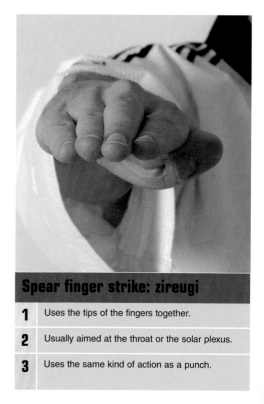

Spear finger strike: zireugi

1	Uses the tips of the fingers together.
2	Usually aimed at the throat or the solar plexus.
3	Uses the same kind of action as a punch.

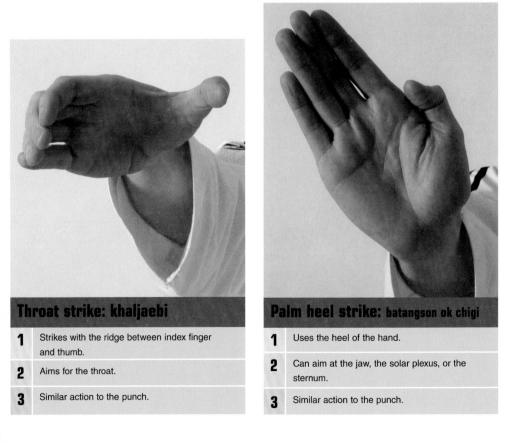

Throat strike: khaljaebi

1 Strikes with the ridge between index finger and thumb.

2 Aims for the throat.

3 Similar action to the punch.

Palm heel strike: batangson ok chigi

1 Uses the heel of the hand.

2 Can aim at the jaw, the solar plexus, or the sternum.

3 Similar action to the punch.

Kicks: chagi

If you look at the cover of most martial arts books and magazines, you will see a picture of somebody doing a kick. If you watch a martial arts film, then the chances are that the exponent will be a "kicker." Indeed, some well-known martial arts actors are renowned for their ability to show high kicks on the film set.

The simple reason for this is that kicks look good. A well-executed kick has an aesthetic quality that hints at the power, balance, and training that the martial artist has worked at.

But kicks are not just there to look good. In practical styles like Tae Kwon Do, nothing is included for aesthetic reasons only. A good kick can be a fast and powerful attack that can cover a long range.

Look at the picture below. Here, one of the Tae Kwon Do students is executing a forward punch. In terms of punching, this is the longest-range punch that there is. But look at the kick (*right*). A simple front kick hits the target and leaves the punching fist in midair.

Now think about the power. Look at the muscles in your arm compared to the muscles in your leg. Most people have at least twice as many muscle in the leg as in the arm.

But a kick is not just about the legs. You should use the whole of your body to drive the power through on a kick. You need to understand what part of the foot you are kicking with and the target area that you can connect to.

The kicks here are some of the basic ones. Nearly all kicks can be done as jumping kicks to give added range and height. Some styles kick with the leading leg for extra speed and others do not.

Kicks are an important aspect of Tae Kwon Do. They help you develop poise and suppleness, and kicking for a few minutes gives good cardiovascular training—any Tae Kwon Do student can vouch for that. However, do not be lured into thinking that Tae Kwon Do is all about kicking. It is but one aspect of a varied art form.

Tae Kwon Do kicks are very powerful and can cover a long range.

Front kick: apchagi

1	contact area	ball of the foot
2	range	long
3	target area	groin, stomach, or chin
4	power	high
5	speed	fast
6	difficulty level	easy
7	suitability for sparring	highly suitable for free sparring

The front kick is fast, powerful, and versatile. It can be aimed at either the stomach (middle section) or the chin (high section) in sparring and can be aimed at the groin and legs in self-defense.

The power of the kick comes from the hip—not just the flick from the knee. The knee is lifted quickly, and the ball of the foot is shot outward in a whiplash type of motion. The foot should travel in a straight line toward the target. As you kick out with the foot, you simultaneously drive the hips forward to generate power. After the kick, it is important to bring the foot back as quickly as you fired it out. This means that your leg cannot be caught so easily.

In the kick, you must use the hips to power the leg. If you can do this, then you will develop great power with your kicks. It is possible to do the front kick as a jumping kick. We will analyze that kick separately.

1. Start in the front stance. Hold your fists to the sides of your body.

2. Lift your knee.

3. Snap the kick outward from the knee and power it from the hips. Pull the foot back quickly.

Front pushing kick: mireo chagi

1	contact area	sole or blade of the foot
2	range	long
3	target area	chest or stomach
4	power	high
5	speed	medium
6	difficulty level	easy
7	suitability for sparring	highly suitable for free sparring in full-contact WTF tournaments

If you have watched a TV drama where somebody kicked a door in, you have seen the pushing kick in action.

The pushing kick is not designed to cause an impact like the front kick or turning kick. The idea of the pushing kick is literally what it says—to push a person. In WTF tournaments, you can gain a point by using a push kick to force your opponent out of the ring.

You could also use the pushing kick to give you the range that you need to follow through with another kick, such as a side kick.

In some respects, the pushing kick is like a front kick. You need to lift the knee and extend the leg. The difference is that with the pushing kick, it is good to lift the knee as high as you can, no matter what the target area is, so that you can drive the kick forward. The foot blade (as in the side kick) or the sole of the foot makes contact with the target.

Several pushing kicks in rapid succession are a common way to knock an opponent out of the ring and gain a point. If more range is required, the distance can be increased with a small hop from the back leg.

1. Start in the fighting stance.

2. Lift your knee high.

3. Thrust the foot forward for the pushing kick. Pull the knee back and step down.

Turning kick: dollyo chagi

1	contact area	ball of the foot
2	range	long
3	target area	head
4	power	high
5	speed	fast
6	difficulty level	medium
7	suitability for sparring	highly suitable for free sparring

The turning kick is very popular in sparring, principally because of its high power and speed. The path of the turning kick is circular, and the attack comes from the side. It is therefore common to try to use it as a high kick to the side of the head. In competition, it is also possible to score a point by kicking to the midsection, if the technique is clean and hits the target properly.

For the traditional turning kick, you will hit with the ball of the foot. This makes the kick very powerful, and this method is sometimes used for breaking boards in demonstrations or gradings.

In sparring and competitions, it is more common to use the instep of the foot. This allows the Tae Kwon Do student to use exactly the same technique, but in a slightly less destructive way. If somebody hits you with the instep of the foot, it will hurt—but not as much as if they used the ball of the foot.

To execute the turning kick, you must lift the knee of the kicking leg and pivot around on the supporting foot. The higher you lift the knee, the higher your kick will be. When you release the kick, power is transmitted from the hips. After the release, you should quickly bring your foot back.

Start in the fighting stance, with your left leg forward.

1. Start in fighting stance.

2. Lift the knee high into the chamber position.

3. Rotate the hips so that the leg becomes parallel to the floor.

4. Snap the foot out and make contact with the ball of the foot for maximum impact.

5. Return the foot to the chamber position.

6. Return the leg to the floor into fighting stance.

There is a reverse version of the turning kick, mom dollyo chagi, (see page 171). It is also possible to do the turning kick as a jumping kick or a jumping and spinning kick.

Axe kick: naeryo chagi

1	contact area	heel or sole of the foot
2	range	long
3	target area	face
4	power	high
5	speed	fast
6	difficulty level	easy
7	suitability for sparring	highly suitable for free sparring in full-contact WTF tournaments

The name for the axe kick is very appropriate. it is performed by raising the leg to a high position and smashing it downward as you would with the stroke of an axe. The power comes from raising the leg high and bringing the straight leg down with force. Make contact with either the heel or the sole of the foot.

It could be used to hit your opponent in the face or smash down on the collarbone. Even in full-contact tournaments, a little care and respect is needed with the kick—you do not really want to break a competitor's collarbone!

Another use for the axe kick is to smash through the opponent's guard. It is straight, direct, and powerful, and, therefore, difficult to block. Sometimes the axe kick is used in this way to clear the target area for another technique.

The axe kick is easy to do and surprisingly effective. It is therefore very popular in tournaments. It is practiced frequently in classes because the kick is also an excellent way of stretching the muscles in your legs to make them more supple.

1. Start in the fighting stance, then raise the leg high.

2. Bring the kick down with the knee straight as hard as you can. Do not slam your foot into the floor—this shows lack of control!

Hook kick: nakka chagi

1	contact area	heel
2	range	medium
3	target area	side of the head
4	power	high
5	speed	fast
6	difficulty level	medium
7	suitability for sparring	highly suitable for free sparring

The hooking kick is very popular with Tae Kwon Do students. It is a very fast and powerful kick, hence its popularity. Different versions are possible, such as the reverse hook kick, making it a powerful and dramatic part of the Tae Kwon Do arsenal of kicks.

It is similar to the turning kick. The difference between the two is that the direction of motion is reversed, and the heel is used to make contact with the target instead of the ball of the foot.

The hook kick is an excellent technique to surprise an opponent. If the opponent sees the hook kick coming, he or she will sometimes think that the kick is the turning kick and react accordingly. If they do this, then the chances are that they will walk straight into the kick, because the direction of motion is reversed. For this reason, it is frequently practiced in combination with the turning kick.

The hook kick is more difficult to execute than some of the front kicks. Most Tae Kwon Do students find it relatively easy because it is practiced so much. In some ways, a good hook kick shows the observer that you practice Tae Kwon Do and not some other martial art that also uses kicks.

1. Start in the fighting stance.

2. Pivot around on your standing leg and extend your kicking leg.

3. Flick the heel back for the kick. Put your foot back on the floor in front of you, and resume the fighting stance.

Side kick: yeop chagi

1	contact area	side edge of the foot
2	range	long
3	target area	knees, stomach, head
4	power	very high
5	speed	fast
6	difficulty level	medium
7	suitability for sparring	highly suitable for free sparring

The side kick is a very powerful kick. In a way, it is like punching with the edge of your foot. The strength of the leg and motion carried through from your body give the kick a powerful piercing quality. The foot must travel in a straight line and make contact with the blade of the foot.

In the Taegeuk Sah Jang routine (see page 216), the target for the side kick is the head.

In sparring, side kicks can be used for straight kicks to the midsection or the head. A useful technique with the side kick is to stop an aggressive attacker. In sparring, some fighters will use attack as the best form of defense. These fighters will sometimes try to rush on to an opponent, making it difficult for him or her to attack. One good way of stopping this sort of attack is with a well-placed side kick. Make sure that your balance is good; otherwise you will just get knocked over!

The side kick can be done from any stance. In it the knee is raised and the kick is delivered by twisting the waist and then thrusting the foot out to its target. As always, you should bring the foot back as quickly as possible after the kick.

The side kick can be used as a jumping kick. With the crescent kick, your foot swings around

1. Start in the fighting stance.

2. Lift your knee in front of your body. Pivot around on your standing leg.

3. Thrust the foot forward with a twist of the hips. Bring the foot back quickly. Put the foot on the floor.

Crescent kick: an chagi

1	contact area	outside of the foot
2	range	long
3	target area	side of the head
4	power	medium
5	speed	fast
6	difficulty level	easy
7	suitability for sparring	highly suitable for free sparring

in an arc. The idea is to try to hit the opponent on the side of the head with your foot. The kick makes contact with the side of the foot.

The crescent kick is quite popular in sparring, as it can sometimes come from the side and take an opponent off guard.

There are many variations of the crescent kick. In the variation shown, the foot travels from outside the body to inside the body (an chagi). It is also possible to do the crescent kick the other way around—traveling from inside to outside (bakkat chagi). With both of these variations, you could also do a jumping kick or a jumping and spinning kick. These are highly aggressive kicks.

The power for the crescent kick comes mainly from the hip and thigh muscles. You use these muscles, reinforced by waist movement to swing the leg in an arc and make the kick.

1. Start in the fighting stance.

2. Shift your weight onto your front leg and lift your back leg.

3. Pivot around on the ball of your standing foot as you make the kick. Put your kicking leg down in front of your body.

Back kick: dwit chagi

1	**contact area**	blade of the foot
2	**range**	long
3	**target area**	stomach
4	**power**	very powerful
5	**speed**	fast
6	**difficulty level**	medium
7	**suitability for sparring**	highly suitable for free sparring

When you execute the back kick, it is easy to put the whole of your body weight behind it, which makes it a very powerful kick.

The back kick feels similar to the sidekick. Be sure that you know the difference if it is in your grading! The big difference is that you will turn through 180 degrees to do a back kick. You make contact with the blade or heel of the foot.

When sparring, the side kick followed by back kick is a good kicking combination. The way that the side kick turns your body means that you only have to turn a little further to perform the back kick.

The back kick can also be done as a jumping kick. This is a more advanced technique, but when mastered, it is very powerful.

1. Start in fighting stance with the weight on the left leg.

2. Rotate the body counterclockwise on the ball of your left foot and pick your right leg up into the chamber position.

3. Thrust out the foot in a straight line to make contact.

4. Return the foot to the floor in front of you.

5. Finish in fighting stance.

Reverse hook kick: mom dollyo chagi

1	contact area	blade of the foot
2	range	long
3	target area	head
4	power	very powerful
5	speed	fast
6	difficulty level	medium
7	suitability for sparring	highly suitable for free sparring

The reverse hook kick is the most difficult kick described in this book. The actual mechanics of the kick are straightforward. You spin your body around and use the momentum to throw the heel of your foot back for the kick.

The difficulty arises in that you have to turn away from your opponent to build up the power. This can make aiming more difficult, especially if the opponent is moving. However, with practice, it can be done very quickly, and exponents of the kick find it highly efficient for scoring points in tournaments.

In tournaments, the flat of the foot is often used. This is obviously to prevent serious injury to your opponent. It is usually aimed at the head of the opponent. For the more powerful kick, the heel of the foot makes contact with the target.

It is possible to do this kick as a jumping kick, but as you can imagine, you will need to be very proficient at the normal version before trying the more advanced jump kick.

As with all kicks, if you want to get it right—all you need is enough practice!

You should make a complete 360-degree turn for this kick, as the momentum of your body turning adds power to the kick.

1. Start in the fighting stance.

2. Spin 180 degrees on the balls of your feet, but fully turn your head to face the opponent.

3. Use the momentum of the spin to throw your leg out.

4. Keep your body moving, and as you get to the target, flick your foot out.

5. After you have made contact, continue rotating.

6. Put your foot on the floor behind you, back in the fighting stance.

Jumping front kick: twio apchagi

1	**contact area**	ball of the foot
2	**range**	very long
3	**target area**	head
4	**power**	high
5	**speed**	fast
6	**difficulty level**	medium to difficult
7	**suitability for sparring**	highly suitable for free sparring

The jumping front kick is spectacular kick and surprisingly easy to execute. As long as you can perform the basic front kick fairly well, then you stand a good chance of succeeding with the jumping front kick. Indeed, an ability to perform the jumping kick may even improve your standing kick technique.

Why jump with a kick? Apart from the aspects of improving your coordination and kicking repertoire, there are good tactical reasons. These are:

1	Height: if you need to get your kicks higher, jump!
2	Distance: some fighters stand well back from an attacker and try to pick their moment. If you are up against one of these, a jumping kick will sometimes give you the range that you need to get at them.

The only difference between the kick for distance and the kick for height is the way that you jump—high or long.

It is possible to do the jumping kick with either the leading leg or the back leg. The basic procedure is just the same.

1. Start in fighting stance.

2. Lift your right knee.

3. Imagine that you are stepping up onto something with your left leg—this gives you the jump. Kick forward with the right foot. Remember to use your hips as well as your knee. Land with your kicking foot forward.

Blocking: makki

Tae Kwon Do attacks are very aggressive. The inner nature of the person should be peaceful, but the defending person will normally respond with an attack that is aggressive and powerful. In Tae Kwon Do, you do not wait for the attacker to just go away. You neutralize an attack and deal with it quickly. Remember that, in a real situation, it is highly possible that there may be more than one attacker. You, therefore, have no time for finesse with the first one because the second one will be on you.

This means that you need a way to deflect or neutralize the attack. This will usually be done by blocking with the forearm, although it is possible to use other parts of the body such as the palm of the hand, feet, knee, or elbow to block an attack. Most of the blocks in Tae Kwon Do are designed to hurt the opponent. If the blocking tools, such as the hands, forearm and knife-hand, are sufficiently conditioned, they can damage the attacker when you perform the block. As such, blocks then become an offensive technique.

Remember that, if you have good footwork, it is better to avoid the attack. In sparring, you should try to use your footwork skills to dodge the attack, only resorting to blocking if you didn't move quickly enough. This is because, if you block a powerful kick, then you are likely to damage your arm. Always consider what you will do after the block.

Blocks can be done to protect the high area (olgul), middle area (momtong), or low area (arae). With the three body areas and other considerations outlined, there is a wide range of blocks available to the Tae Kwon Do student. We shall examine some in the pages that follow.

The high block is a powerful blocking technique used to protect the head.

Low block: arae makki

This is probably the most basic Tae Kwon Do block. For this reason, it is usually taught to the Tae Kwon Do student very early in the training.

The block uses the outer forearm to strike the opponent's attack and knock it out of the way. You will often see this block done in the front stance. It can also be done in any of the other stances.

A typical application for this block would be to defend against a lower front kick as shown. Do not get stuck with this idea. What is to stop you from using exactly the same technique as a lower hammer fist strike to the opponent's inside leg or groin?

When blocking, do not try to hit your opponent's fist or foot, as it is too easy to miss that target. It is better to use the block against the opponent's forearm or lower leg—larger targets—which will ensure successful application of the block.

The low block defends against a turning kick.

1. Start in the ready stance.

2. Point your right fist downward and raise your right fist to your ear as you start to step forward.

3. Drive your right arm down and pull your left arm back as you step. Finish with a twist of the hips in the front stance, extending your right arm into the lower block. Your fist finishes just in front of your leg, not on the outside.

High block: olgul makki

The second of the basic Tae Kwon Do blocks is the high block or olgul makki. Where the previous block protects the lower abdomen and groin area, this block protects the head.

It can be used to protect against a kick or a punch coming toward your face as shown.

The basic sequence for the upper block is as follows.

1. Start in the ready stance.

2. Step forward with your left leg into the front stance and raise your right arm—this will be your reaction arm.

3. Lift your left fist into the blocking position, remembering to pull the reaction arm back.

4. Sink into the front stance as you twist your waist, thus forcing the left arm up into the blocking position. Your right arm should snap back to your waist. Try to do this movement powerfully.

Outer block: bakkat makki

So far, we have looked at defending the head area and the lower groin area. Obviously, we need to look after the midsection as well!

The two most basic blocks for the middle section are the inward block and the outward block.

Torsion of the waist and the correct timing of the reaction hand generate the power for the inner and outer blocks. Rotation of the forearm at the end of the block adds power in the same way that rotation of your fist at the end of a punch gives power.

The outer forearm block makes contact with the opponent's outer forearm using the (side of the small finger), whereas the inner forearm block makes contact with the inner forearm, using the side of the thumb.

The outward block is useful because it tends to "open up" the attacker, ready for your counter-attack.

1. Start in the ready stance.

2. Point your right fist downward and raise your right fist to your ear as you start to step forward.

3. Drive your right arm down and pull your left arm back as you step. Finish with a twist of the hips in the front stance, extending your right arm into the lower block. Your fist finishes just in front of your leg, not on the outside.

Inner block: an makki

This block works in a similar way to the previous one. Instead of opening the opponent, it can be used to force the opponent's attack to cross his or her own body. This makes it difficult for the opponent to follow with another attack, and you still have plenty of target areas that you can hit.

In this block, we use the outside of the forearm (on the side of the little finger) to knock the opponent's attack out of the way. Another application of this block could be to use it like a hammer fist strike to the temple. The mechanics would be just the same; you will just aim a little higher and change the focus of your mind from blocking to striking.

The steps for the block are as follows.

1. Start in the front stance with your right leg forward and your right arm in the lower blocking position.

2. Step forward with your left foot, placing it close to your right foot as you extend your right arm. Raise your left fist behind your head.

3. Pull your left arm back as your right arm starts to come down. Your left foot steps forward. Sink into the front stance as you snap the right arm down into the blocking position and your left arm back to your waist.

Reinforced forearm block: kodureo momtong makki

So far, we have looked at the four basic blocks in Tae Kwon Do. There are, however, many more blocks available to the Tae Kwon Do student. Other blocks include knife-hand blocks, the X-block, the pressing block, and reinforced forearm blocks.

Some of these blocks are shown in the section on Tae Kwon Do poomsae (routines). If you can understand the basic idea and the mechanics of these four blocks, along with the basics of punching, you should have little difficulty seeing how the other blocks work and assessing their individual tactical advantages.

One block that is slightly outside the frame of the others is the reinforced forearm block. It is unusual because you actually use both arms to block on one side.

If you are up against a powerful kicker, then sometimes a simple one-armed block will not have the strength to stop a full-on turning kick. Obviously, it would have been a better idea to not let the kick happen or be out of its way, but life is not always like that!

In this situation, use the reinforced forearm block. It is similar to the outward block, but the fist of the non-blocking arm touches your forearm just inside the elbow. This makes the block much more rigid because it is supported by your other arm.

Although the block is very strong, you still have to be careful with your timing and aim. If you let the kicker aim a full-force turning kick at your forearm when it is supported in such a way, it will probably stop the kick but might damage your arm at the same time. Use your understanding of the kick to try to hit the leg in a safer place.

Start in the front stance with your right leg forward and your right arm in the lower blocking position.

1. Step forward with your left foot, placing it close to your right foot as you raise your right arm.

2. Raise your left fist to a position near your right inner elbow.

3. Step forward as you push outward with your left fist. Your right fist moves very little.

4. Sink into the front stance as you snap the left arm across and your right fist flicks up so that your left fist touches your inner forearm.

Chapter 7 **Poomsae**

Poomsae are a fixed sequence of movements intended to teach the basic principals of Tae Kwon Do, without the use of an opponent. From a technical viewpoint, poomsae *is* Tae Kwon Do. Kyorugi (sparring) is the practical application of Tae Kwon Do.

Tae Kwon Do students learn and practice attacking and defensive techniques against an imaginary opponent using a series of movements. It is important that each movement is performed as it would be performed in reality. Constant repetition of the poomsae, or moves, conditions your body so that each movement will become effective, if you should really need to defend yourself.

Poomsae enable students to increase their breathing control, flexibility, balance, strength, and understanding of power application.

The Taegeuk Poomsae were established so that students could learn the basic philosophical principals of Tae Kwon Do. Each poomsae has its own meaning, and the movements of each poomsae should reflect the meanings of each of the forms.

Taegeuk poomsae

Yin and yang symbolize the great cosmic forces that are equal but opposite. The forces are perpetually cycled to attain harmony and balance. The Taegeuk symbol represents the principle that everything in the universe is created and develops through interactions between the yin (negative) and yang (positive) forces, such as hard and soft, or heavy and light. The circumference of the Taegeuk symbolizes the infinity of the two opposite forces. The circle is divided equally into a red upper section that represents the yang, and the lower blue section that represents the yin.

The eight bar signs (called Kwae) outside the circle come from the *Yu Yeok* (the Korean version of the Chinese I Ching or *Book of Changes*). The Kwae signify the progression of yin and yang through a spiral of change and growth. One bar represents the yang, while two bars represent the yin principals. The three unbroken bars symbolize heaven-creative (keon), while the opposite three broken bars symbolize earth-receptive (kon). Each Kwae is represented by a pattern of the Taegeuk poomsae.

The Taegeuk showing the eight Kwae.

Poomsae	Kwae symbol	Kwae name	Kwae meaning
Il Jang		Keon	Heaven: light, creation, and the yang.
Yi Jang		Tae	Joy: inner firmness and the outer softness.
Sam Jang		Ri	Fire: sun and warmth.
Sah Jang		Jin	Thunder: great power and dignity.
Oh Jang		Seon	Wind: gentle, but penetrating.
Yuk Jang		Kam	Water: formless, yet never loses its nature.
Chil Jang		Kan	Mountain: "op stop" stability, unmoveable.
Pal Jang		Kon	Earth: pure yin, receptive, where the creative force of Keon is realized.

Improving your poomsae

Here are some of the things to look out for.

Body alignment

Is your body aligned in the most efficient way? If your front stance leans to one side, for example, you cannot deliver the maximum power. The laws of physics will be against you because gravity will always try to pull you into your worst direction. If a body is in alignment, the energy meridians are open, and Ki can flow.

Balance

This feeds back into the first concept of body alignment. If your body is aligned, then it is balanced. But it is not just about your body. If your mind and body are not balanced, then you are not balanced physically. An example here is thinking about the next technique before you finish the one you are executing. You may begin to lean into the technique, thus upsetting the alignment and balance of the first one.

If your technique is correct and you are striking or blocking to the correct parts, you are starting to control your body with your mind.

Smooth breathing and powerful deliveries are indicators that you have started to balance internal and external factors.

No mind

Balance leads straight into the concept of "No Mind" or "the empty space." In poomsae, you should think about the movement that you are on—not the one you just did or the one about to come. This means that you need to be balanced between the past and the future. This is what the meditation experts call the "here and now." Learning to experience the moment as it is leads to a profound state of meditation, and poomsae can help you to get there.

The Tae Kwon Do student must show very high spirit and an extreme level of alertness. The power of the kihap and the focus of the eyes are clear indicators that the spirit is strong.

Each movement should be performed as proficiently as possible.

The patterns: poomsae

The steps for all the Taegeuk Poomsae follow the same basic pattern (see right). Phonetic symbols of the Korean alphabet are used to describe the position and direction of movement of the practitioner. The Tae Kwon Do student starts at position Na and moves forward (toward Ga) or backward (toward Na) along a vertical line. Movements to the left of the starting point are indicated by Da, while movements to the right are indicated by Ra.

In all the Tae Kwon Do poomsae, the performer must execute each technique with realism, as though responding to an attack from an opponent. The head should always turn first to look at the imaginary opponent before performing the technique. The eyes should always pierce straight into the eyes of the opponent and not down onto the floor.

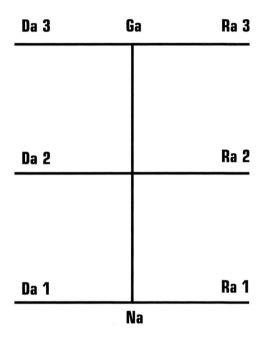

Da 3	**Ga**	**Ra 3**
Da 2		**Ra 2**
Da 1		**Ra 1**
	Na	

Taegeuk II Jang

Taegeuk II (one) Jang represents the Kwae symbol of Keon and means heaven, light, creation, and the Yang. This poomsae represents the force of creation by containing the most basic of Tae Kwon Do movements composed to accommodate white belt students. It consists largely of walking stance (apseogi) but involves a shift to the front stance (apkubi). Movements include the low block (arae makki), inside midsection block (momtongmakki), middle punch (momtong jireugi), and front kick (ap chagi). These basic techniques are used throughout the practice of Tae Kwon Do.

1. From the Na position look toward Ga in ready stance (kibon jumbi seogi).

2. Turn counter-clockwise to the left in the direction of Da1, place your left foot along the line of Da1 in a left walking stance (apseogi) and simultaneously execute a low block (arae makki) with the left hand.

3. Step forward and place the right foot in the direction of Da1 in a right walking stance (apseogi) and execute a mid-section punch (momtong bandae jireugi) with the right hand.

4. Turn in a clockwise direction by pivoting on the ball of the left foot and place your right foot in the direction of Ra1 in a right walking stance (apseogi) and simultaneously execute a low block (arae makki) with the right hand.

5. Step forward in the direction of Ra1 into a left walking stance (apseogi) and execute a midsection punch (momtong bandae jireugi) with the left hand and place your right foot in the direction of Ra1 in a right walking stance (apseogi). Simultaneously execute a low block (arae makki) with the right hand.

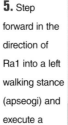

6. Turn counter-clockwise by pivoting on the ball of the right foot and place your left foot in the direction of Ga in a left front stance (apkubi). Simultaneously execute a low block (arae makki) with the left hand.

7. Keeping the feet as they are, immediately execute a mid-section reverse punch (momtong baro jireugi) with the right hand.

8. Turn in a clockwise direction by pivoting on the ball of the left foot and place your right foot on the line of Ra2 in walking stance (apseogi). Simultaneously execute a reverse inward midsection block (momtong anmakki) with the left hand.

9. Step forward and place your left foot on the line of Ra2 in walking stance and deliver a midsection reverse punch with the right hand.

10. Turn counterclockwise and move your left foot in the direction of Da2 in walking stance; perform a reverse inward midsection block with the right hand.

11. Step forward in the direction of Da2 in walking stance (ap seogi) and deliver a midsection reverse punch (momtong baro jireugi) with the left hand.

12. Turn clockwise and place the right foot in the direction of Ga in a right front stance and execute a low block (arae makki) with the right hand.

13. Keep the feet as they are and immediately execute a midsection reverse punch (momtong baro jireugi) with the left hand.

14. Pivot counterclockwise and step forward with your left foot to Da3 in a walking stance; do a high-section block with the left hand.

15. Execute a front kick (apchagi) with the right foot.

16. Place the foot toward Da3 and execute a mid-section punch (momtong bandae jireugi) with the right hand.

17. Pivot clockwise on the ball of your left foot and face the direction of Ra3 in walking stance (apseogi) and execute a high block (olgul makki) with your right hand.

18. Deliver a front kick (apchagi) with the left foot and place the foot in the direction of Ra3 in walking stance (apseogi).

19. Execute a midsection punch (momtong bandae jireugi) with the left hand.

Front view

Front view

20. Pivot clockwise on the ball of the right foot and place your left foot in the direction of Na in a left front stance and execute a low block with the left hand.

21. Step forward with your right foot in the direction of Na in front stance (apkubi) and execute a midsection punch with the right hand with a loud kihap.

22. End (keuman) by pivoting counterclockwise on the ball of the right foot, moving the left foot to the right, turn to face the direction of Ga and return to ready stance.

Application of Taegeuk Il Jang
Sequence 1: application of movements 2 & 3

Movement 2: the attacker delivers a front kick (apchagi). The defender blocks it with a low block (arae makki).

Movement 3: the defender immediately steps forward to counter-attack with a punch to the stomach (momtong bandae jireugi).

Sequence 2: application of movement 6

Movement 6: the attacker delivers a front kick (apchagi). The defender blocks the kick with a low block (arae makki). He immediately follows by counter-attacking with a reverse punch (baro jireugi) to the stomach.

Sequence 3:
application of movements 14 & 15

Movement 14: the attacker delivers a punch to the head (olgul jireugi). The defender blocks the punch with a high block (olgul makki).

Movement 15: the defender counter-attacks using a front kick (apchagi).

This is followed by a punch to the stomach (momtong bandae jireugi).

Taegeuk Yi Jang

Taegeuk Yi (two) Jang represents the Kwae symbol of Tae, which means joy and signifies inner firmness and the outer softness. Tae is feminine and is symbolized by the image of a lake, so it is not aggressive and is of a spiritually uplifting nature. This poomsae should be performed with ease and fluidity, but firmly with control. This poomsae introduces punching toward the head of the opponent and the high block.

1. From the Na position look toward Ga in ready stance (kibon jumbi seogi).

2. Turn counterclockwise to the left in the direction of Da1, place your left foot along the line of Da1 in a left walking stance (apseogi) and simultaneously execute a low block (arae makki) with the left hand.

3. Step forward and place the right foot in the direction of Da1 in a right front stance (apkubi). Execute a midsection punch (momtong bandae jireugi) with the right hand.

4. Turn in a clockwise direction by pivoting on the ball of the left foot and place your right foot in the direction of Ra1 in a right walking stance (apseogi) and simultaneously execute a low block (arae makki) with the right hand.

5. Step forward in the direction of Ra1 into a left front stance (apkubi) and execute a midsection punch (momtong bandae jireugi) with the left hand.

6. Pivot counter-clockwise on the ball of your right foot and place your left foot one step forward into a walking stance in the direction of Ga and execute a reverse inward midsection block (momtong anmakki) with the right hand.

7. Step forward into walking stance (apseogi) in the direction of Ga and execute a reverse inward midsection block (momtong anmakki) with the left hand.

8. Rotate counterclockwise on the ball of your right foot and place the left foot in the direction of Da2. Execute a low block (arae makki) with the left hand.

9. Step forward and place the right foot in the direction of Da1 in a right front stance (apkubi) and execute a mid-section punch (momtong bandae jireugi) with the right hand.

11. Pivot clockwise on the ball of your left foot and place your right foot one step forward in the direction of Ra2 in a right walking stance (apseogi) and execute a low block (arae makki) with the right hand.

10. Execute a punch to the head (olgul bandae jireugi) with your right hand.

12. Perform a front kick (apchagi) with the left foot and place the foot one step forward in the direction of Ra2 in front stance (apkubi).

13. Execute a punch to the head (olgul bandae jireugi) with your left hand.

14. Rotate counter-clockwise on the ball of your right foot and place the left foot in the direction of Ga in a left walking stance (apkubi) and perform a high block (olgul makki) with the left hand.

15. Step forward and place the left foot in the direction of Ga into a right walking stance (apseogi) and perform a high block (olgul makki) with the right hand.

16. Rotate counter-clockwise on the ball of your right foot and take your left foot into the direction of Ra3 in a right walking stance (apseogi) and execute an inward middle block (momtong anmakki) with the right hand.

17. Move your right foot a little in the direction of Da3 and rotate clockwise on the ball of left foot to face the direction of Da3 and execute an inward middle block (momtong anmakki) with the left hand.

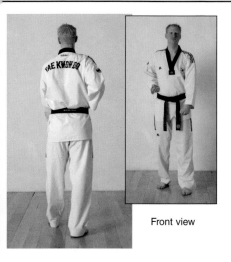

Front view

18. Rotate counterclockwise on the ball of your right foot and place the left foot in a left walking stance, (apseogi) facing the direction of Na, and execute a low block (arae makki) with the left hand.

Front view

19. Execute a front kick (apchagi) with the right foot and place the foot one step forward in the direction of Na into a right walking stance (apseogi).

Front view

20. Deliver a midsection punch (momtong bandae jireugi) with the right hand.

Front view

21. Execute a front kick (apchagi) with the left foot and place the foot one step forward in the direction of Na into a left walking stance (apseogi).

Front view

22. Deliver a midsection punch (momtong bandae jireugi) with the left hand.

Front view

24. Deliver a midsection punch (momtong bandae jireugi) with the right hand with a loud shout (kihap).

Front view

23. Execute a front kick (apchagi) with the right foot and place the foot one step forward in the direction of Na into a right walking stance (apseogi).

25. End (keuman) by keeping the right foot at the Na position, rotate counterclockwise on the ball of your right foot to face the direction of Ga, and move the left foot into ready stance (kibon jumbi seogi).

Application of Taegeuk Yi Jang
Application of movements 18–24.

Movement 18: the attacker delivers a front kick (apchagi) and the defender deflects the kick with a low block (arae makki).

Movement 19: the defender counter-attacks by delivering a front kick (apchagi).

Movement 20: he follows with a midsection punch (momtong bandae jireugi).

Movement 21: the defender pursues the attacker and performs a second counter-attack delivering a front kick (apchagi).

Movement 22: this is followed by a midsection punch (momtong bandae jireugi).

Movement 23: the defender performs a third counter-attack, delivering a front kick (apchagi).

Movement 24: this is followed by a midsection punch (momtong bandae jireugi).

Taegeuk Sam Jang

Taegeuk Sam (three) Jang represents the Kwae symbol of Ra, which means fire, sun and warmth. Ri is feminine. Movements of this poomsae should be performed emulating the qualities of fire with flickering energy. Like fire, this poomsae contains changing bursts of power connected with a continuous flow of movements. Moves combined in quick succession include front kicks followed immediately with a double punch, a front kick followed by a low block and reverse punch and a single knife-hand block followed with a reverse middle punch. This poomsae introduces outward middle blocks with the knife-hand, the knife-hand strike and back stance.

1. From the Na position look toward Ga in ready stance (kibon jumbi seogi).

2. Turn counter-clockwise to the left in the direction of Da1, place your left foot along the line of Da1 in a left walking stance (apseogi), and simultaneously execute a low block (arae makki) with the left hand.

3. Execute a front kick (apchagi) with the right foot and place the foot one step forward in the direction of Da1 into a right front stance (apkubi). Simultaneously execute a low block (arae makki) with the left hand.

4. Instantly follow the front kick by a midsection double punch (momtong dubeon jireugi), punching with the right hand first.

i

ii

5. Rotate clockwise on the ball of your left foot, place the foot one step forward in the direction of Ra1 in a right walking stance (apkubi), and execute a low block (arae makki) with the right hand.

6. Execute a front kick (apchagi) with the left foot and place the foot one step forward in the direction of Ra1 into a left front stance (apkubi).

7. Instantly follow the front kick with a midsection double punch (momtong dubeon jireugi), punching with the left hand first.

8. Rotate counterclockwise on your right foot stepping toward Ga with your left foot into a left walking stance (apseogi) and execute a right knife-hand strike (hansonnal jebipoom mokchigi) with the right hand.

9. Step forward toward Ga with your right foot into walking stance (apseogi) and execute a knife-hand strike (hansonnal jebipoom mokchigi) with the left hand.

10. Turn counterclockwise and move the left foot in the direction of Da2 in back stance (dwit kubi) on your right leg; perform an outward knife-hand middle block with the left hand.

11. Immediately after the knife-hand block, keep the right foot fixed and push the left foot forward half a step towards Da2 into front stance and deliver a reverse punch (momtong baro jireugi) with the right hand.

12. Keep the left foot fixed, pivot clockwise on the ball of your right foot to face the direction Ra2 in back stance (dwit kubi) and execute an knife-hand outward middle block (hansonnal momtong yopmakki) with the right hand.

13. Immediately after the knife-hand block, keep the left foot fixed and push the right foot forward half a step towards Ra2 into front stance (apkubi) and deliver a reverse punch with the left hand.

14. Pivot counterclockwise on the ball of the right foot and place your left foot one step forward toward Ga in walking stance (apseogi) and execute a reverse inward middle block (momtong anmakki) with the right hand.

15. Step forward toward Ga with the right foot into walking stance (apseogi) and execute a reverse inward middle block (momtong anmakki) with the left hand.

16. Pivot counterclockwise on the ball of your right foot and move your left foot toward Ra3 into a left walking stance (apseogi) and execute a low block (arae makki) with the left hand.

17. Execute a front kick (apchagi) with the right foot toward Ra3 and place the foot forward into a right front stance (apkubi seogi).

18. Follow the front kick instantly by a mid-section double punch (momtong dubeon jireugi), punching with the right hand first.

19. Pivot counterclockwise on the ball of your left foot and move your right foot toward Da3 into a right walking stance (apseogi) and perform a low block (arae makki) with the right hand.

20. Execute a front kick (apchagi) with the left foot toward Da3 and drop the foot forward into a left front stance (apkubi seogi).

21. Immediately follow the front kick by a midsection double punch (momtong dubeon jireugi), punching with the left hand first.

Front view

Front view

Front view

22. Pivot counterclockwise on the ball of your right foot moving the left foot toward Na into a left walking stance (apseogi) and deliver a low block (arae makki) with the left hand.

23. Follow immediately with a reverse middle punch (momtong baro jireugi) with the right hand without changing the stance.

24. Step forward with your right foot toward Na into a right walking stance (apseogi) and execute a low block (arae makki) with the right hand.

Front view

25. Follow immediately with a reverse middle punch (momtong baro jireugi) with the left hand, without changing the stance.

Front view

26. Deliver a front kick (apchagi) with the left foot and drop the foot toward Na into a left walking stance (apseogi).

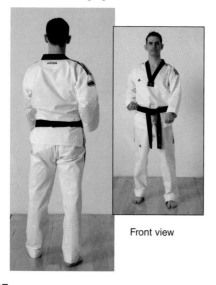

Front view

27. Deliver a left low block (arae makki).

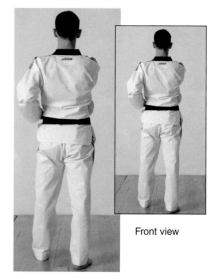

Front view

28. Immediately follow with a reverse middle punch (momtong baro jireugi) with the right hand, without changing the stance.

Front view

Front view

29. Deliver a front kick (apchagi) with the right foot and drop the foot toward Na into a right walking stance (apseogi).

30. Deliver a low block (arae makki) with the right hand.

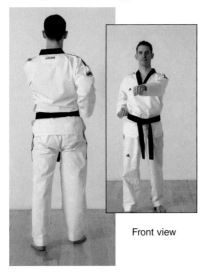

Front view

31. Immediately follow with a reverse middle punch (momtong baro jireugi) with the left hand, without changing the stance and add a loud kihap.

32. End (keuman) by pivoting counterclockwise on the ball of the right foot to face the direction of Ga and bring your left foot to the right into ready stance (kibon jumbi seogi).

Application of Taegeuk Sam Jang
Sequence 1: application of movements 2 & 3.

Movement 2: the attacker delivers a turning kick. The defender blocks the turning kick with a low block (arae makki).

Movement 3: the defender counter-attacks by delivering a front kick (apchagi).

Immediately followed by a double punch (dubeon jireugi) to the stomach.

Sequence 2: application of movements 8 & 11.

Movement 8: The attacker delivers a punch (momtong jireugi). The defender deflects the punch with an outward knife-hand middle block (hansonnal momtong yopmakki) in back stance.

The blocking arm immediately grabs the attacker's arm and pulls the attacker off balance.

Movement 11: the defender counter-attacks by shifting his weight from the back to the front leg into front stance (apkubi seogi). He delivers a reverse punch (momtong baro jireugi).

Taegeuk Sah Jang

Taegeuk Sah (four) Jang represents the Kwae symbol of jin, which symbolizes thunder with great power and dignity. Thunder evokes fear and trembling, but once this has passed there is a feeling of being refreshed. In the face of danger it is necessary to act calmly, with the knowledge that the danger will eventually subside. Find the courage to face fear so that the thunderstorm may nourish the soul.

This poomsae introduces many new techniques including knife-hand techniques and two side kicks (yeop chagi) in combination.

1. From the Na position look toward Ga in ready stance (kibon jumbi seogi).

2. Turn counter-clockwise to the left in the direction of Da1, place your left foot along the line of Da1 into a back stance (dwit kubi) with your right leg back and perform a twin knife-hand block (sonnal momtongmakki).

3. Pull the right foot forward toward Da1. As you are stepping, perform a middle section pressing block (nullomakki) with the left hand.

5. Pivot clockwise on the ball of your left foot and move your right foot to face the direction of Ra1 into a back stance (dwit kubi) with your right leg back and perform a twin knife-hand block (sonnal momtong makki).

4. Finish the move in a right front stance (apkubi seogi) and deliver a spear finger thrust (pyonsonkkeut sewo tzireugi) to the middle with the right hand.

6. Pull the left foot forward toward Da1. As you are stepping, perform a middle section pressing block (nullomakki) with the right hand.

7. Finish the move in a left front stance (apkubi seogi) and deliver a spear finger thrust (pyonsonkkeut sewo tzireugi) to the middle with the left hand.

8. Pivot counterclockwise on the ball of your right foot, moving the left foot toward Ga into a left front stance (apkubi seogi) and perform a high knife-hand block with the left hand, while simultaneously performing a knife-hand strike with the right hand to the neck (jebipoom mokchigi).

9. Deliver a front kick (apchagi) with the right foot and drop the foot forward toward Ga into front stance (apkubi seogi).

10. Execute a reverse punch to the middle (momtong baro jireugi) with the left hand.

11. Perform a side kick (yeop chagi) with the left foot and drop your foot toward Ga into a front stance (ap kubi).

12. On completion of the side kick (yeop chagi), immediately perform another side kick (yeop chagi) with the right foot.

13. Drop your foot forward toward Ga into a back stance (dwit kubi) with your left foot back and perform a twin knife-hand block (sonnal momtongmakki).

14. Rotate counterclockwise on the ball of your right foot and move your left foot forward toward Ra3 into a back stance (dwit kubi) with your right leg back and perform a outward middle block (momtong bakkat makki) with the left hand.

15. Perform a front kick (apchagi) with the right foot and drop the foot back to its original position into back stance (dwit kubi).

16. Perform a reverse inward middle block (momtong anmakki) with the right hand. The body should be twisted 45 degrees toward the opponent during this block.

17. Keep both your feet in the same position, but rotate clockwise to face the direction of Da3 in back stance with the left leg back and perform a outward middle block (momtong bakkat makki) with the right hand.

Front view

18. Perform a front kick (apchagi) with the left foot and drop the foot back to its original position into back stance (dwit kubi).

19. Perform a reverse inward middle block (momtong anmakki) with the left hand. When performing this block, the body should be twisted 45 degrees toward the opponent.

20. Keeping the right foot fixed, move the left foot toward Na into front stance and simultaneously perform a high knife-hand block with the left hand and a knife-hand strike to the neck (jebi poom mokchigi).

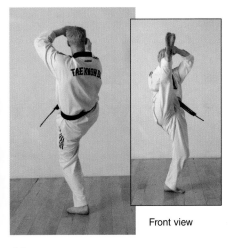

Front view

Front view

21. Perform a front kick (apchagi) with the right foot and drop the foot one step forward toward Na into front stance (apkubi seogi).

22. Deliver a right back-fist strike to the face (deungjumeok apchigi).

23. With the right foot fixed, rotate counterclockwise while moving the left foot to face the direction of Ra2 in a left walking stance (apseogi) and perform an inward middle block (momtongmakki) with the left hand.

24. Keep the feet fixed and perform a reverse middle punch (momtong baro jireugi) with the right hand toward the direction of Ra2.

25. Keep the feet fixed but rotate clockwise to face the direction of Da2 in walking stance (apseogi) and deliver a inward middle block (momtongmakki) with the right hand.

Front view

26. Keep the feet fixed and perform a reverse middle punch (momtong baro jireugi) with the left hand toward the direction of Da2.

27. Keep the right foot fixed, rotate counter-clockwise, and move the left foot to the direction of Na into a left front stance (apkubi seogi). Then, perform an inward middle block (momtongmakki) with the left hand.

28. Immediately deliver a double punch (momtong dubeon jireugi) to the middle starting with the right hand.

Front view

Front view

29. Move your right foot forward in the direction of Na into a right front stance (apkubi seogi) and perform an inward middle block (momtong makki) with the right hand.

Front view

30. Immediately deliver a double punch
(momtong dubeon jireugi) to the middle, starting
with the left hand with a loud kihap.

31. End (keuman) by
keeping the right foot
fixed and rotating the
body counterclockwise to
face the direction of Ga
into ready stance (kibon
jumbi seogi).

Application of Taegeuk Sah Jang
Sequence 1: application of movements 2, 3, & 4

Movement 2: the attacker punches (momtong bandae jireugi) the opponent. The defender deflects the punch using a twin knife-hand block.

Movement 3: the attack continues with a second punch (momtong baro jireugi), which is deflected using a pressing block (nullomakki).

Movement 4: the defender counter-attacks using a spear finger strike (pyonsonkkeut sewo tzireugi) to the stomach.

Sequence 2: application of movements 11 & 12

Movement 11: the defender attacks using a side kick (yeop chagi) to the opponent.

Movement 12: the defender pursues the opponent and delivers a second side kick (yeop chagi).

Sequence 3: application of movements 20, 21 & 22

Movement 20: the defender counter-attacks the
opponent's high punch (olgul jireugi) by
performing a high knife-hand block and
simultaneously attacking the opponent with a
knife-hand strike to the neck (jebipoom
mokchigi).

Movements 21 and 22: the defender continues the counter-attack by
applying a front kick (apchagi) while grabbing and pulling the
opponent's wrist using the hand that has just performed the high block
and applying a back-fist strike (deungjumeok) with the other hand.

21

22

Chapter 8 Kyorugi or sparring

One of the useful things about poomsae is that you can train on your own. You can work a little each day on the poomsae and ask your instructor to correct any imperfections.

Poomsae training on its own would be very one-dimensional and would certainly not reflect the true spirit of Tae Kwon Do. To understand a technique, you need to practice it with somebody else. Practicing Tae Kwon Do with a partner is called "kyorugi," which translates closely to the word "sparring."

Kyorugi is done on different levels. The first level involves three punches from an attacker. In this, the attacking person will make three steps.

The defender will respond by blocking each punch and will deliver a counter-attack on the final attack (three-punch kyorugi). This approach teaches Tae Kwon Do students how to distance themselves and to become accustomed to the idea of an attacker.

One variation of attacking three times is for the attacker to deliver one single punch (one punch kyorugi). In one punch kyorugi the attacker will counter-attack immediately after the first attacking punch. The emphasis here is on power, speed, and accuracy. You must be able to demonstrate that you are attacking the chosen target accurately and not attacking aimlessly.

The attacks and defenses are done as though they are real, although there is no actual contact. The fact that both Tae Kwon Do students understand the situation gives them the chance to use full speed and power.

Sparring is also a form of kyorugi. Tae Kwon Do students try to attack each other to score points. This gives them the chance to test themselves against each other. It is an excellent technique for sharpening the skills and is the technique used for sport Tae Kwon Do.

We will now examine some examples of sparring.

Three punch kyorugi

Three punch kyorugi is often called "three-step sparring." This is the most basic form of kyorugi. Clubs train using different techniques in their syllabus, but the basic concept is always the same. This training is a controlled way of blocking three punches from an attacker. Once the attacker has performed the last punch, the defender retaliates with a counter-attack. Here are some examples of three punch Kyorugi. These examples should be useful for you to get the idea.

1. Start in the attention stance—charyot seogi.

2. Bow (kunyeh).

3. Go into to ready stance (jumbi seogi). (Steps 1 and 2 are only done at the start of training with a new partner).

4. In front stance the attacker delivers a punch. The defender retreats into back stance and blocks using momtongmakki.

5. The attacker delivers a second punch, while the defender steps back and blocks a second time.

6. The attacker steps forward and punches a third time while the defender steps back and blocks a third time.

7. After the third block, the defender slides his right foot forward into front stance and delivers a reverse punch (baro jireugi) with a loud kihap (shout).

One punch kyorugi

One punch Kyorugi is often called "one-step sparring." This is similar to three punch Kyorugi except that the defender counter-attacks after one punch, rather than waiting for three punches. If you are stuck for techniques, try using techniques in the poomsae. All the techniques used in the poomsae are realistic and can be applied the self-defense situation. It is always good to experiment—that way you can make your own mistakes and learn in a more effective way. Always remember to perform the attack and counter-attack (defense) using both sides of the body. It is important to practice all techniques, using both the left and right feet and hands.

Here are four examples:

Example number 1

Defense using a foot sweep.

1. Start in ready stance: jumbi seogi.

2. The attacker steps forward into front stance and delivers a straight punch. The defender steps back into tiger stance and performs an inward block (momtongmakki).

3. The defender rotates on the ball of the left foot and knocks the attacker's leg away.

4. As the attacker falls to the ground, the defender finishes the technique by punching to the head with a loud kihap (shout).

Example number 2

Defense by blocking using a kicking technique

1. Start in ready stance: jumbi seogi.

2.The defender anticipates the attack and so steps back into fighting stance.

3. The defender blocks by using a crescent kick to the hand.

4. The defender then performs a side kick (yeop chagi) with a loud kihap (shout).

5. The defender returns to fighting stance.

Example number 3

Close fighting defense using the palm, knee and elbow as weapons

1. Start in ready stance— jumbi seogi.

2. The defender blocks the attacker's punch by stepping forward and using a reverse knife-hand block.

3. The defender grabs the attacker's wrist and immediately strikes the attacker using a palm strike.

4. The defender continues by striking the stomach with the knee.

5. The defender finishes the technique by jumping and performing a downward elbow strike to the back with a loud kihap (shout).

Example number 4 Defense using a foot sweep and arm break

1. Start in ready stance—jumbi seogi

2. The defender blocks the attack using a reverse block.

3. Immediately, the defender strikes the attacker's chin using an elbow strike.

4. The defender steps through with the left leg . . .

5. . . . and sweeps the attacker to the floor. Note that the defender is holding the attacker's arm with his right hand.

6. The defender punches the attacker with the left hand . . .

7. . . . and then grabs the attacker's arm with the right hand.

8. The defender then breaks the attacker's arm using his shin as a lever. . .

9. . . . and continues the motion until the attacker is facing downward. Place the knee on the shoulder and pull the attacker's hand back so that he can't move his arm.

Variations of one punch kyorugi

1 Instead of attacking from front stance, try attacking from ready stance. This makes the training more realistic as nobody would punch you from front stance in reality.

4 Attack by punching to the head rather than the body.

5 When defending perform a different counter-attack for either side of the body.

6 Attack using both body and head punches to add more realism to the training.

In WTF full-contact kyorugi, protective clothing must be worn.

Sparring

So far, all the poomsae and kyorugi techniques that we have looked at apply Tae Kwon Do techniques in a controlled way. Such training "programs" your body and mind into a set of responses. If an attack comes, you do not need to think about your response, you just do it.

Sparring is the aspect of Tae Kwon Do where you test those responses. In sparring, you get the opportunity to test your skills.

Sparring is not a "free for all." To avoid injury, very strict guidelines should be followed. Respect for your training partner is paramount. Under no circumstances should the fighter lose control of their aggression. The Tae Kwon Do students who become angry and try to hurt an opponent are showing how little they understand about their training.

Sparring is popular because it can be used as a sport. It should be remembered that spar-

ring is only a small part of Tae Kwon Do training. Anyone who trains only to enter Tae Kwon Do competitions without developing the other aspects taught in the Tae Kwon Do syllabus are not true students of Tae Kwon Do. By definition, sport has winners and losers—it is a competition. In reality, there are no "winners" or "losers" in a fight.

If you are sparring and your partner gets through your defenses, think about it positively. How did it happen? Can he do it next time? How do I stop him? Every time your partner penetrates your defenses, he or she has taught you something. Try not to let your ego get in the way—learn from the experience.

In a Tae Kwon Do class, the most advanced form of free sparring is where two Tae Kwon Do students are simulating a fight situation in a continuous practice fight. It is very different from real fighting in that there are rules. These rules are essential for the safety of the Tae Kwon Do student. It is a mark of respect to both your fellow Tae Kwon Do student and all that have gone before you in Tae Kwon Do that the rules are not broken.

1	**No strikes below the belt.**
2	**No strikes to vital areas such as the neck, kidneys or groin.**
3	**No strikes to the joints—elbows or knees.**
4	**Always wear groin protection and a gum shield.**
5	**Show respect for your partner—if you are more advanced than your partner, it is not an excuse for you to give him or her a bad time.**
6	**If the instructor shouts "Kalyeo," you must stop what you are doing immediately. This rule is highly important and overrides anything else that may be happening in the Dojang.**

If executed with respect for your fellow Tae Kwon Do student, free sparring is an energetic and highly enjoyable way of learning Tae Kwon Do. Just remember, you are there to LEARN, not to win.

WTF is full contact, so by definition, contact cannot be excessive. Head gear is always used when performing full-contact sparring.

Two competition fighters trying to find an opening in their opponent's guard.

The attacker delivers an axe kick (naeryo chagi) to the head.

Side kick (yeop-
chagi) to the
chest.

The turning kick is one
of the most common
techniques used in
competitions. The
attacker has faked a
low kick, thereby
causing the defender
to drop his guard. The
attacker then delivers a
turning (dollyo chagi)
kick to the head.

The attacker's turning kick (dollyo chagi) to the head is blocked by the defender.

The side kick is a very powerful kick. The best defense against such kicks is to avoid them. Here, the defender has stepped away from the kick.

Learning techniques for kyorugi

When you start to learn free sparring, you will usually be in the situation where you are training with more advanced Tae Kwon Do students than yourself. These people are here to help you. Most of them can remember what it felt like to be a beginner and how ferocious a high section side kick can appear.

Use the situation. Remember that the more advanced student will not be perfect either. If you see an opening, take it but keep your control. A frequent beginner's mistake is to see an opening and not show control. Remember that your sparring partner may have some tricks left up the sleeve of his or her Dobok!

The following exercises are also excellent for practicing your sparring.

1 **ATTACK OR DEFENSE ONLY**
One person attacks, while the other evades or blocks the technique. This is a practice technique where one Tae Kwon Do student will be on the attack and the other will dodge or block the technique. This forces the defender to be very sharp with the evasions and defense.

2 **ONE KICK SPARRING**
This is very similar to normal free sparring. As long as you are within the rules of your Dojang for sparring, you are encouraged to use any suitable technique. The difference between sparring and one kick sparring is that you take turns to attack. One person attacks, while the other evades the attack and immediately follows with a single technique, and so it goes on. Since there is not normally any contact in this type of training, it is an excellent way of building up speed and stamina and trying out difficult techniques.

Kyorugi competitions

Unlike many other martial arts, Tae Kwon Do contests are full contact. For this reason, sparring competitions are physically very demanding. The Tae Kwon Do contestant must have enough physical resilience to endure powerful attacks to the body and head. Mental agility is also important, as a lapse in concentration will probably mean that points will be scored against you, or else you will miss opportunities to score points. For reasons of safety, only a limited range of Tae Kwon Do techniques are permitted in competitions.

Conditions of entry to competitions

Contestants must hold the nationality of the team that they are representing. To compete in WTF competitions, contestants must be a member of the World Tae Kwon Do Federation.

Contestants are required to wear a Tae Kwon Do uniform (Dobok).

Contestants are required to wear protective equipment. Compulsory protective equipment includes a head guard, gum shield (white or translucent), body protector (also called a "hogu"), groin guard (male and female), forearm protector, and shin guards (not instep).

Contestants are not permitted to wear glasses, jewelry, scarves, or anything else likely to cause injury.

The use of any drugs is prohibited. Tae Kwon Do is an Olympic sport, and so drugs or chemical substances described by the IOC (International Olympic Committee) are prohibited.

The tournament

A Tae Kwon Do match is controlled by a referee who also assures compliance with the rules and assesses penalty points for violations of the competition rules. Four corner judges score the match by recording all scores and penalties. Points must be scored by at least two of the four corner judges. The Head of Court presides over the ring as chief official. His job is to ensure that all decisions made by the referee and corner judges are as fair as possible. The Head of Court decides on the point scores based on the score sheets submitted by corner judges at the end of each round. Refereeing officials should not come from the same country or club as either of the contestants.

Due to the full-contact nature of Tae Kwon Do competitions, body weight can give the contestant a big advantage or disadvantage. To eliminate any weight bias, contestants are "weighed in" prior to the fight to determine which weight

	category	male division	female division
1	**fin weight**	not exceeding 110 lbs (50 kg)	not exceeding 95 lbs (43 kg)
2	**fly weight**	110 lbs (50 kg) to 120 lbs (54 kg)	95 lbs (43 kg) to 104 lbs (47 kg)
3	**bantam weight**	120 lbs (54 kg) to 128 lbs (58 kg)	104 lbs (47 kg) to 112 lbs (51 kg)
4	**feather weight**	128 lbs (58 kg) to 141 lbs (64 kg)	112 lbs (51 kg) to 121 lbs (55 kg)
5	**light weight**	141 lbs (64 kg) to 154 lbs (70 kg)	121 lbs (55 kg) to 132 lbs (60 kg)
6	**welter weight**	154 lbs (70 kg) to 168 lbs (76 kg)	132 lbs (60 kg) to 143 lbs (65 kg)
7	**middle weight**	168 lbs (76 kg) to 183 lbs (83 kg)	143 lbs (65 kg) to 154 lbs (70 kg)
8	**heavy weight**	over 183 lbs (83 kg)	over 154 lbs (70 kg)

Contestants wear either a blue (chung) or red (hong) hogu (body protector) so that the judges can distinguish between them.

Tae Kwon Do sparring competition consists of three rounds. For men, each round is three minutes with a one-minute rest period between rounds. For women and juniors, the duration of each round is shortened to two minutes. The number and length of rounds may vary according to the rules of a particular tournament, if time is a limiting factor. Matches are fought in a 12 meter-by-12 meter competition area, which is normally on a high-density foam rubber mat.

To start the contest, the contestants turn to the Head of Court and bow. The contestants then turn to each other and exchange a bow at the referee's command. The referee will then start the contest by commanding "Shijak" (begin). The referee may break the bout by command of "Kalyeo." The contest is stopped by the command "Keuman."

To win a Tae Kwon Do competition, the contestant must score more points (duek-jeom) than the opponent. Additionally, the contest may be won if the opponent is disqualified, the opponent withdraws from the fight, the opponent is unable to continue the bout, or if a decision of superiority is made by the referee. If a knockout occurs due to prohibited techniques, the victim is the victor of the contest.

To score a point, the strike must be delivered to the target area of the body or head. The strike must cause a "trembling shock," i.e., delivered with sufficient power to abruptly displace the target. The target area for punching is restricted to the front part of the hogu. The target area for kicking is the front and sides of the head and the hogu. An attack to the hogu scores one point, whereas a kick to the head scores two points. Additionally, a point is scored if the opponent is knocked down. Points do not stop the action

unless there is a knockout or someone is pushed out of the ring. The match can continue if the opponent recovers by the referee's count of eight. If the referee's count goes past eight, the contestant will lose by knockout.

Point deductions and warnings are made against prohibited techniques. This ensures that the competition is safe and fair. Many dangerous techniques are prohibited from the Tae Kwon Do match for the contestants' safety. In the event of a warning, the referee will deduct half a point from the contestant's score. A full deduction indicates the loss of one point.

Warnings (Kyong-go or penalty) are awarded for grabbing the opponent; pushing the opponent with the shoulder, hands, or arms; holding the opponent with the hands or arms; intentionally crossing the 8m alert line; evading by turning the back to the opponent; intentionally falling down; feigning injury; attacking the knee; intentionally attacking the groin; hitting the opponent's face with the hands or fist; gesturing to indicate scoring; uttering undesirable remarks; or any misconduct on the part of the contestants or coach.

Deductions (Gam-jeom or penalties) are awarded for attacking the fallen opponent; intentionally attacking after the referee has stopped the contest; intentionally attacking the back or back of the head; severely attacking the opponent's face with the hand or fist; head-butting; crossing the 12m boundary line; throwing the opponent; or violent or extreme behavior from the contestant or the coach.

If the contestant refuses to comply with the rules, the referee may declare him or her the loser. Also, if a contestant reaches –3 points, the contestant will be declared the loser.

In the event of a tied score, the Head of Court will instruct the referee to make a superiority decision. The referee will take the following into account: which contestant technically dominated the other, used a greater number of techniques, used more advanced techniques, or displayed the best competition manner. If the determination of the tied score involves a tie through the deduction of penalty points, the competitor who scored more points will win.

Breaking

In any martial art, techniques must be effective. Breaking tests the power of the practitioners' techniques. In addition to simply breaking boards, the technique is often combined with highly choreographed gymnastics.

In order to have the ability to break boards without injury, the martial artist must condition the striking area. One way of preparing your knuckles for destructive techniques is to perform push-ups on the knuckles used for punching. Punching bags are also an effective way of developing knuckle hardness. The feet are con-ditioned by training barefoot.

When breaking boards, it is necessary to determine where the broken pieces are going. Shattered wood could easily injure a member of the audience. Broken material should also be cleared up to prevent injury during the demon-stration. Do not break with a head-butt as this can easily cause brain damage. While children's bones are developing, they are softer than those of adults and can easily be damaged by destructive techniques.

Korean language

Nobody is expecting you to become a linguist if you start to learn Tae Kwon Do. In many clubs, the names for the movements are called out in Korean.

One reason for this is that if you understand the Korean name for a technique, then you will understand it in any part of the world you may be training in. So, you can even practice Tae Kwon Do on your vacation!

Another good reason to be acquainted with the Korean names is that it is a traditional Korean art. Why not learn the names that Tae Kwon Do has given to its own techniques, rather than those given by some interpreter?

Korean is generally written in "Hanguel," an alphabet developed during King Sejong's reign in the 15th century. Hanguel contains 24 characters. This glossary covers some of the words and phrases used in Tae Kwon Do. Since the Korean language does not use the English alphabet, translation often causes variation in spellings.

Counting

1	one	hana	il
2	two	dul	yi
3	three	set	sam
4	four	net	sah
5	five	daseot	oh
6	six	yeoseot	yuk
7	seven	ilgop	chi
8	eight	yeodeol	pal
9	nine	ahop	gu
10	ten	yeol	sip

An chagi	Crescent kick
An makki	Inward block
Anpalmok makki	Blocking from the inside of the body to outside using the inside part of the forearm
Apchagi	Front kick
Apchigi	Face back fist
Apkubi seogi	Front stance
Apseogi	Walking stance
Arae	Low section
Arae makki	Low block
Bakkat chigi	Outer back fist strike
Bakkat makki	Outward block
Bakkat palmok makki	Blocking from the inside of the body to outside using the outside part of the forearm
Bandae jireugi	Punching with the same side as the leading leg
Baro jireugi	Punching with the opposite side to the leading leg (reverse punch)
Batangson teok chigi	Palm heel strike
Beom seogi	Cat stance
Bit chagi	Half-turning kick
Chagi	Kicking
Chigi	Striking
Chi jireugi	Uppercut punch
Chireugi	Thrusting
Deungjumeok	Back fist
Deungjumeok apchigi	Back fist strike to the face
Dobok	Tae Kwon Do uniform
Dojang	Tae Kwon Do training hall
Dollyo chagi	Turning kick (Roundhouse kick)
Dollyo jireugi	Hooking punch
Dubeon jireugi	Double punch
Dwit chagi	Back kick
Dwit kubi	Back stance

Hansonnal jebipoom mokchigi	Knife-hand strike
Hansonnal momtong makki	Single knife-hand block from the inside of the body to outside
Hansonnal momtong yopmakki	Knife-hand block from the inside of the body to outside (outward middle block)
Jebipoom mokchigi	High knife-hand block and high knife-hand strike in the same move
Jireugi	Punching
Joochoom seogi	Horse riding stance
Jumeok	Jumeok
Keuman	End
Khaljaebi	Throat strike
Kibon jumbi seogi	Ready stance
Kihap	Shout
Kodureo momtong makki	Reinforced forearm block
Kongkyok kisul	Attacking techniques
Kup (or Gup)	Grades of Tae Kwon Do proficiency below black-belt level
Makki	Blocking
Mejumeok chigi	Hammer fist strike
Mireo chagi	Front pushing kick
Mom Dollyo chagi	Reverse turning kick
Momtong	Body
Momtong anmakki	Block from outside of the body to inside using the outside of the forearm and the reverse hand (reverse inward midsection block)
Momtong bakkat makki	Outward middle block
Momtong bandae jireugi	Body punch (midsection punch)
Momtong baro jireugi	Body punch with the reverse hand (midsection reverse punch)
Momtong dubeon jireugi	Midsection double punch

Momtongmakki	Block from outside of the body to inside using the outside of the forearm (inward block)
Naeryo chagi	Axe kick
Nakka chagi	Hook kick
Nullomakki	Pressing block
Olgul	Face/High section
Olgul babdaejireugi	High punch
Olgul makki	High block
Palkoop	Elbow
Palkup dollyo chigi	Inside elbow strike
Palkup dwiro chigi	Reverse middle elbow strike
Palkup ollyo chigi	Upper elbow strike
Pyonsonkkeut sewo tzireugi	Spear finger thrust
Seogi	Stance
Sonnal	Knife-hand
Sonnal bakkat chigi	Inside knife-hand strike
Sonnal deung chigi	Reverse knife-hand strike (or ridge hand)
Sonnal mok chigi	Outside knife-hand strike
Sonnal momtong makki	Twin knife-hand block
Twio ap chagi	Jumping front kick
Tzireugi	Spear finger strike
Yeop chagi	Side kick

Further reading

The Lonely Planet Guide to Korea,
Lonely Planet Publications, Melbourne, 2001

Kuk-kiwon Tae Kwon Do Textbook
O Sung Publishing Company

State of the Art Tae Kwon Do
Brandon Saltz (1993)

Tae Kwon Do Vol.1
Kim Jeong-Rok (1986)

Sport Stretching
Michael J. Alter (1990)

Your Personal Trainer
Fulcher and Fox (2002)

Brudnak, M.A., Dundero, D., Van Hecke, F.M. (2001)
"Are the hard martial arts, such as the Korean martial
art of Tae Kwon Do, of benefit to senior citizens?"
Medical Hypothesis 59 (4), 485–491.

Cheuvront, S.N., Carter, R.N., Sawka, M.N. (2003)
"Fluid balance and endurance exercise performance."
Current Sports Medicine Reports 2, 2002–208.

Toskovic, N.N. (2001) "Alterations in selected
measures of mood with a single bout of dynamic Tae
Kwon Do exercise in college-age students."
Percept Motor Skills, 92: 1031–8.

Kurian, M, Caterino, L.C., Kulhavy, R.W. (1993)
"Personality characteristics and duration of ATA Tae
Kwon Do training."
Percept Motor Skills, 1993; 76(2): 363–6.

index

Credits & acknowledgements

Mark Pawlett: I would like to thank my Tae Kwon Do instructors of the past, present, and future. I was inspired to take up the art of Tae Kwon Do in my early teens by Master T. Slaney, my first instructor. Master Slaney trained my second instructor, D. Porter (thanks for the bruises Dennis). I would also like to thank Masters Q. Khan (London Tae Kwon Do Association) and C. Lees (Stevenage Tae Kwon Do).

The author and publishers would also like to thank the following people for taking part in this book:

MASTER FORAN

Master Foran holds a 5th Dan Black Belt in Tae Kwon Do, and 1st Dan Black Belt in Kempo Karate and The Arnis De Mano system of Escrima, and has trained for eight years in Kickboxing and Hap Ki Do.

Master Foran was awarded a commendation award in the local community for his work helping bullied children to make better decisions for their futures, to become more confident, and to say no to unhealthy peer pressure. Master Foran was British Tae Kwon Do Champion three times, and International Gold Medallist three times.

The award-winning Chris Foran Black Belt Schools teach the No.1 Martial Arts curriculum in the UK and have been offering instruction and training in Tae Kwon Do since 1996. Located in Middlesex, UK, Chris Foran Black Belt Schools have produced champions in life as well as in the martial arts. www.chrisforan.com

MRS. FORAN

Mrs. Foran holds a 3rd Dan Black Belt in Tae Kwon Do, a 1st Dan in The Arnis De Mano system of Escrima, and has eight years experience in martial arts including Kickboxing. Mrs. Foran is a great teacher and is trained specifically to work with junior students.

Mrs. Foran is one of the most successful female Tae Kwon Do players in the UK, and has a natural ability when competing at technical competitions and as a fighter.

MR. TULLY

Mr. Tully has been involved in Martial Arts for 25 years and is a 2nd Dan in Tae Kwon Do. He is dedicated to the continuing development and improvement of his 300 students. Mr. Tully is also a certified instructor in the Arnis De Mano system of Escrima and Clash of the Titans Champion.